*This book is dedicated to my two children, Guthrie and Maisie,
who had the sometimes blessing and probably many times
misfortune of having a psychologist for a mother.
I got to try out all my theories on you!*

About the Author

 Susan Weinschenk is a Ph.D. behavioral psychologist. She applies research in psychology and neuroscience to business situations. Dr. Weinschenk is the Founder and Principal of the Weinschenk Institute. She consults with Fortune 1000 companies, educational, government, and non-profit organizations. Her clients call her "the brain lady" because she reads and interprets the latest research in neuroscience and how the brain works, and applies that research to business and everyday life. Susan writes a blog for *Psychology Today* called "Brain Wise: Work better, work smarter", and also has a blog at her website: www.theteamw.com/blog

Susan started college at Virgina Tech and finished her undergraduate degree in Psychology at Northeastern. She then earned a Masters and Ph.D. at Pennsylvania State University.

Susan lives in Wisconsin, USA, with her husband. Her two children are grown and "launched." When she's not working, she performs in community theatre, sings jazz, reads books, watches movies, and bakes artisan breads.

Visit the book website at www.theteamw.com/books

Other books by Susan Weinschenk:
- *100 Things Every Presenter Needs to Know about People* (New Riders, 2012)
- *100 Things Every Designer Needs to Know about People* (New Riders, 2010)
- *Neuro Web Design: What Makes them Click?* (New Riders, 2008)

How to Get People to Do Stuff

Master the art and science of
persuasion and motivation

Susan M. Weinschenk, Ph.D.

VOICES THAT MATTER™

How To Get People to Do Stuff:
Master the art and science of persuasion and motivation

Susan M. Weinschenk, Ph.D.

New Riders
www.newriders.com

To report errors, please send a note to errata@peachpit.com

New Riders is an imprint of Peachpit, a division of Pearson Education.

Copyright © 2013 by Susan M. Weinschenk, Ph.D.

Project Editor: Michael J. Nolan
Production Editor: Tracey Croom
Development Editor: Jeff Riley/Box Twelve Communications
Copyeditor: Gretchen Dykstra
Proofreader: Jennifer Needham
Indexer: Joy Dean Lee
Cover & Interior Designer: Mimi Heft
Compositor: David Van Ness

ISBN 13: 978-0-321-88450-3
ISBN 10: 0-321-88450-7

5   17

Printed and bound in the United States of America

Contents

Chapter 6

Instincts   **95**

Chapter 7

The Desire for Mastery   **109**

Chapter 8

Tricks of the Mind   **123**

Chapter 9
Case Studies: Using Drivers
and Strategies in the Real World   161

Chapter 10
The Strategy List   **187**

Acknowledgements

Research in psychology has a rich history. I am grateful to all the researchers and psychologists whose work I am describing in this book, including Ivan Pavlov, B.F. Skinner, B.J. Fogg, Daniel Kahneman, Timothy Wilson, and Robert Cialdini, just to name a few. Look at my reference list and you'll see everyone whose research contributed to this book.

Thank you to my blog readers and clients who submitted case study situations that they wanted answers to.

Thanks go to Michael Nolan at New Riders for his continual encouragement of my book ideas and his great advice, and to Jeff Riley. This is book #4 with this team. Who would have thought we'd do all these books together?

The Seven Drives

DO YOU COOK? Are you good at it? I like to think I am, and sometimes the things I cook turn out great; other times not so wonderful.

I learned to cook from watching my mom cook, following recipes, and experimenting on my own. Recently I got a book about the science of cooking. Now I'm learning why some recipes work and others don't, or why some of my substitutions are not a good idea.

Instead of having to follow a recipe slavishly, or experimenting on my own and wondering what's going to happen, I now can apply what I know about the science of cooking—about what chemicals in food react with others to make food flavorful or tender. I can still give it my own flair, but given a particular situation with a particular set of ingredients, I can apply what I know about the science of cooking to create a great meal.

Now let's apply this principle to people.

Are you good with people? Do you know how to get them to do stuff? Are you using tips and techniques you picked up from others or experimented with? If so, I bet that, like my cooking before I studied the science, sometimes your strategies work and other times they don't.

What if you understood the science behind what motivates people? If you understood the science and knew how to apply it to a particular person or group of people in a particular situation, you would be able to get people to do stuff. You wouldn't have to guess at what strategy to use—you'd know.

That's what this book will do for you.

The 7 Drivers of Motivation

My children, who, as I write this, are grown adults, have often accused me of using my psychology skills on them when they were growing up. And they're right!

I knew that it was working when my daughter, at age three, was whining about something she wanted, and my five-year-old son looked at her and said, "Haven't you learned yet that you don't get anything you want in this family by whining?" She stopped. His statement was accurate.

Having been a psychologist for over 10 years by the time I had children, I was determined to use what I knew about psychology to raise children who would not whine (and would be flexible, and compassionate, and hardworking, and so on). But especially children who would not whine. I hated whining!

I did have the benefit of being able to work with my children from the time they were born. I don't have that advantage with everyone else I interact with. But I've learned that if you understand what motivates people, then you can change and modify what you do, what you offer, and how and what you ask of people. You can change your strategies and tactics to get people to do stuff.

Empirical research in psychology goes back over 100 years. Some of the original work still holds true. The ability to peer into the brain and watch it work, which is now possible, has proved some of those original findings to be correct, and has given us many more insights into what makes people tick. I've used the original, foundational research in this book, as well as the newest findings.

This book describes seven drives that motivate people:

- The Need to Belong
- Habits
- The Power of Stories
- Carrots and Sticks
- Instincts
- The Desire for Mastery
- Tricks of the Mind

In the book I'll describe each drive, explain the research behind it, and then give you specific strategies to use.

The Need to Belong

Did you see the movie *Cast Away*? Tom Hanks's character is on a plane that crashes on an island in the South Pacific. He lives there alone for several years. He takes a volleyball, paints a face on it, and talks to it constantly. It's a Wilson brand volleyball, and Hanks ends up calling his "friend" Wilson. Without real people to interact with, he had to create someone.

We are ultimately social animals, and our desire to connect with others is a strong, innate drive. We're not meant to live alone, and we'll work hard to be socially accepted. We need to feel that we have a place in the world where we belong.

You can use the need to belong, and the longing for connectedness, to get people to do stuff.

Habits

It might surprise you to learn how much of everything we do in a typical day we do out of habit without even thinking about it. We don't even remember how those habits got formed.

I'll bet that you tend to wash yourself the same way each time you take a shower, and that you have your own personal morning ritual. How did these habits come to be?

If so much of what we do in a day is made up of habits we formed without realizing it, why does it seem so hard to change habits or create new ones?

We hear so much about how it takes months to create a new habit. How could that be, when we seem to have created hundreds of them easily without even realizing it? It turns out that it's actually very easy to create a new habit or even change an existing one, if you understand the science behind habit formation.

You can use this knowledge to help other people create or change habits, so you can get them to do stuff.

The Power of Stories

What kind of person are you? Are you someone who helps those in need? Do you keep up on the latest trends and fashions? Are you a family person who spends time and energy to nurture family relationships?

We all have self-personas. We tell ourselves and others stories about who we are and why we do what we do. Some of our self-personas and our stories are conscious, but others are largely unconscious.

We like our self-personas to be consistent. Feeling that we're being inconsistent makes us uncomfortable.

If you understand what stories people tell themselves about who they are, then you can communicate in a way that matches those stories and thereby get people to do stuff.

Carrots and Sticks

Have you ever been to a casino? Think about this: You spend a lot of time and energy trying to get people to do stuff; you may even offer rewards or pay people to do stuff. And yet a casino gets people to pay them!

Casinos understand the science of reward and reinforcement. They use what's called a "variable ratio schedule" to get people to play again and again and again, even if the person is losing money.

You can use what the casinos know. You can apply the research on the different schedules of rewards and when to use which one, as well as why using rewards directs behavior better than punishment does.

Years ago, psychology was dominated by the study of rewards, or reinforcements. Now we know that other drives, such as instinct, mastery, and the need to belong are often stronger and more motivating than rewards. But, there are times when using a reward is the best way to get people to do stuff.

There's a right way and a wrong way to use rewards. You need to know the right way to get people to do stuff.

Instincts

Imagine you're driving down the road and there's an accident ahead. You tell yourself not to slow down and look, and yet you feel the irresistible urge to do exactly that.

We sometimes forget that if we're human then we're members of the animal kingdom. We have certain basic instincts that are part of each of us. These instincts include survival, the search for food, and the drive for sex. These instincts are strong and largely unconscious. They affect our behavior. Sometimes you can get people to do stuff just by tapping into these instincts.

For some of you, using the desire for sex or food might not be appropriate or relevant to what it is you want people to do. But the survival instinct is one that is constantly operating, and can be used to get people to do stuff.

The unconscious is constantly scanning the environment to keep us safe and alive. This means that we're particularly susceptible to things that are unexpected, and things that make us afraid. Fear of loss is a huge motivating factor. You can tap into these instincts to get people to do stuff.

The Desire for Mastery

Even stronger than giving an external reward is the desire for mastery. People are very motivated to learn and master skills and knowledge.

This is called intrinsic motivation, because the motivation is internal to the person, in contrast to giving rewards, which is an extrinsic motivation. Intrinsic motivations are usually more powerful than extrinsic ones. Because a desire for mastery is intrinsic you can't exactly get someone to be motivated by it, but you can pay attention to the situation overall.

Certain situations encourage a desire for mastery, and others dampen the desire for mastery. You can use what we know from the research on mastery to set up conditions that will encourage and stimulate the desire for mastery, and, by doing so, get people to do stuff.

Tricks of the Mind

You've probably seen visual illusions—where your eye and brain think they're seeing something different than they really are. What you may not realize is that there are cognitive illusions, too. There are several biases in how we think. Our brains are wired to jump to quick conclusions. This is useful in reacting quickly to our environment, but sometimes these fast conclusions and decisions lead to cognitive illusions.

Did you know that if you mention money, people become more independent and less willing to help others? Or that people tend to filter out information they don't agree with, but that you can get past those filters?

You can use the idea of cognitive illusions to get people to do stuff.

Too Manipulative?

When I give talks or interviews on how to get people to do stuff, the question of ethics often comes up: "If we use this information from psychology to get people to do stuff, are we being too manipulative? Is it ethical?"

This is something I've spent a lot of time thinking about. It's not an easy issue to deal with.

Some say that if you're trying to get people to do something, no matter what it is, then that *is* unethical. Others say that if you're trying to get people to do something that's good for them (eat healthier, quit smoking), then it's OK. I fall somewhere between these two ideas.

The first thing to understand is that you can't actually get people to do stuff unless, on some level, they want to do it. You can encourage people to do stuff, you can set up situations where their own motivations and drives will kick in, but you don't have total control. The goal is to get people to want to do the stuff that *you* want them to do.

Getting people to think before they act, encouraging people to behave in ways that serve society as a whole (conserve energy, be kind to others, donate money to worthy causes)—these are OK in my opinion, and most people agree with me. But what about getting people to buy something?

Having recently served as an expert witness/consultant for the US government on cases involving Internet fraud, I have a better feel for where the line is on ethical and unethical behavior. Putting your product or service in its best light and matching your product or service with the needs and wants of your customers—these are OK in my opinion.

Does everyone really need a new refrigerator? Probably not. But encouraging them to buy a new refrigerator now, and to buy it from you, is perfectly fine in my opinion. (Otherwise we might as well proclaim that all marketing and advertising is unethical.)

Purposely deceiving people, providing confusing instructions so people don't know what they've agreed to, encouraging people to engage in behavior that harms themselves or others, or trying to get people to break the law—these are not OK in my opinion.

Here's what I keep in mind: "to do good or to do no harm."

Assuming I haven't scared you off with ethical concerns, I hope you're ready to master the seven drivers of motivation. In the following chapters, you'll learn the research behind and details of each. And then with a little practice, some trial and error, and a willingness to keep an open mind and learn from your mistakes, you'll become a master of how to get people to do stuff.

2

The Need to Belong

IF I ASK YOU TO THINK of a time when you felt like you didn't belong, you can probably think of at least a few, and maybe many.

Perhaps you remember being a child and not being picked for a team during a game at school. Or maybe you can recall a time as a teenager when some other teens who you thought were your friends didn't invite you to a party. Maybe you've had a more recent event that left you feeling that you didn't belong. Perhaps you've walked into a room at work and everyone there was younger or older than you and they were discussing a mutual topic of interest, like a game or sports event that you knew nothing about.

Each situation probably made you feel like you didn't belong. It's likely that this feeling of not belonging also made you feel sad, lonely, depressed, or angry.

Now think of a time when you felt that you *did* belong. Perhaps you had a special group of friends in school, or you remember feeling very close at family events. Or maybe you felt a sense of belonging while watching a football game with other fans.

These experiences of belonging were probably accompanied by feelings of well-being and happiness.

We have a strong need to feel that we belong. We will take actions in order to feel that we belong in a group. We will avoid actions that make us feel ostracized from a group that is important to us. The need to belong is powerful and it affects us more than we may realize.

When People Feel Connected, They Work Harder

Gregory Walton is a professor at Stanford who has studied the important effects of belonging on behavior (Walton 2012). In one of his experiments, Walton found that when college students believed they shared a birthday with another student, they were more motivated to complete a task with that student and performed better on the task.

He found the same effect with four- and five-year-olds. In another study Walton had people who were part of the experiment jog in place, raising their heart rate. Participants in the study who felt they were socially connected to the jogger (for example, were told they had the same birthday) had an increased heart rate, too. Walton concluded that it's easy for people to take on the goals, motivations, emotions, and even physical reactions of people whom they feel even minimally connected to.

In other research Walton found that when people feel they are working with others as a team to reach a goal, they are more motivated to achieve the goal, even without any extrinsic reward, than if they are working alone. They work harder and longer at the task, become more absorbed, and perform better.

Again, this is true with both adults and children.

STRATEGIES

Strategy 1: Get people to feel connected to others and they will work harder.

Use Nouns, Not Verbs

The need to belong can have very subtle effects. We identify ourselves in terms of the groups we belong to and this sense of group can deeply affect our behavior.

You can stimulate group identity just by the way you have people talk about themselves or the way you phrase a question. For example, Gregory Walton's research shows that if people say "I am a chocolate eater" versus "I eat chocolate a lot," it affects the strength of their preference for chocolate. "Eater" is a noun. "Eat" is a verb. People who say "I am a chocolate eater," who use the noun instead of the verb, show a stronger preference for chocolate.

In a survey about voting, Walton's experimenters asked, "How important is it to you to be a voter in tomorrow's election?" versus "How important is it to you to vote in tomorrow's election?" When the noun (voter) was used instead of the verb (vote), more people actually voted the following day. Feeling that you belong to a specific group affects your behavior.

When you ask people to do stuff, use nouns rather than verbs. Invoke a sense of belonging to a group and people are much more likely to comply with your request.

STRATEGIES

Strategy 2: When you ask for something, use nouns to invoke group identity rather than verbs.

Harness the Power of Others' Opinions

Have you ever attended a church or religious service that was not one you were used to? You're not sure what's going to happen next. People are responding or praying or singing or chanting. They're sitting, or standing, or kneeling at various cues. You surreptitiously steal glances at everyone around you and try to imitate what they're doing. If everyone stood up and put paper bags on their heads and turned around three times, you probably would look to see where your paper bag was.

Why is the behavior of others so compelling? Why do we pay attention to and copy what others do? It's called *social validation*.

In an experiment from the 1970s, research participants would go into a room, supposedly to fill out a survey on creativity. In the room would be one or more other people, pretending they were also participants, but who were really part of the experiment. Sometimes there would be one other person in the room, sometimes more. While people were filling out their creativity survey, smoke would start to come into the room from an air vent. Would the participant leave the room? Go tell someone about the smoke? Just ignore it?

Bibb Latané and John Darley (Latané 1970) conducted this experiment and many others like it. They set up ambiguous situations to see if people were affected by what those around them were or were not doing. What action, if any, the participant took depended on the behavior of the other people in the room, as well as how many other people there were.

The more people in the room, and the more the others ignored the smoke, the more the participant was likely to do nothing. If the participant was alone, he or she would leave the room and notify someone within a matter of seconds. But if there were others in the room who didn't react, then the participant would do nothing.

We like to think that we're independent thinkers, that we're unique individuals. The truth is, however, that the need to fit in and belong is wired into our brains and our biology. We want to fit in. We want to be like the crowd. This is such a strong drive that when we're in a social situation, we look to others to see how to behave. It's not a conscious process; we don't know we're doing it. People are most likely to look to others if they're uncertain what to do.

You can use social validation to get people to do stuff. It's easy and powerful—provide information on how many other people are doing the very thing you want them to do.

For example, if you want people to quit smoking, tell them how many other people (in this program, in this country, in the world, in a particular time frame, with this method) have quit smoking. If you want people to buy a product, tell them how many people have already purchased it. If you want them to donate money, tell them how many people have already donated.

Obviously this works only if a significant number of people have already done the behavior you are looking for.

Make sure you don't unintentionally tell people how many people have done something that you *don't* want them to do. It's a bad idea to let teenagers know that 25 percent of teens smoke or binge drink. Sometimes people or organizations give out this message in order to highlight how big a problem there is.

CHANGING ENERGY USE WITH NEIGHBOR COMPARISONS

Some energy companies are using the power of social validation to get people to use less energy. They send customers a rating that shows their energy use on a chart, compared with their neighbors. If the customer has used less energy than the average of their neighbors, there's a smiley face. They tried using a frowning face when the energy use was more than the neighbors', but got negative feedback about that, so customers either get one smiley face, two smiley faces (if they really saved a lot of energy), or no smiley face if they did not do better than their neighbors, or if they did much worse than their neighbors. People consistently saved more energy when they could compare their energy usage with their neighbors' in this way (Allcott 2011).

For example, I was at a college orientation meeting for parents and incoming college students. One of the college administrators said that in the previous three years there were over 200 violations of the alcohol regulations in the dormitories on campus. He was pointing out that they had an alcohol problem on campus. He then went on to talk about all the ways they were trying to deal with the problem. But the damage of his message was already in place: he had just told a room of 300 incoming students that many of the other students were drinking. It's likely that statement caused *more* drinking, not less.

Before you make your argument about why people should do the stuff you want them to do, do your research and get some data on how many people are already doing it.

 STRATEGIES

Strategy 3: To get people to do something, show them that others are already doing it.

Make Sure the Right Person Does the Asking

You're at a fundraiser. Someone gets up to make a short speech and asks everyone at the event to donate money for a special project.

Which of the following is true?

a. You're more likely to donate money if the speaker is similar to you in characteristics such as age and dress.

b. You're more likely to donate money if you find the speaker attractive.

c. You're more likely to donate money if the speaker is different from you.

d. Neither attractiveness nor similarity will affect your decision to donate.

e. Both b and c.

f. Both a and b.

The correct answer is f. You're more likely to donate if the speaker is similar to you in characteristics such as age and dress and if you find the speaker attractive.

You might be thinking, "Well, other people might be affected by such superficial considerations, but not me." But we're all affected by what someone looks like. And our decisions about whom to talk with, whether to believe or listen to them, and whether to do what they're asking of us are definitely affected by the cues that tell us whether the person is "like" us and whether the person is "attractive" to us.

Sometimes the way to get people to do stuff is to make sure the right person is doing the asking. Research shows that we have different reactions to different people.

The Brain Has a Special Response to People You Know

Your friend David asks you to consider sponsoring him for a 10K run he's doing to raise money for his favorite charity. Will you sponsor him? What if it's a friend of David's whom you don't know, but you know they are friends? What if a stranger asks you to sponsor him for the race? Are you more or less likely to say yes for these different people?

What if your cousin Frank asks you? And what if you and Frank are polar opposites? At every family gathering you and Frank end up arguing about politics. Would you be more or less likely to say yes to Frank if he asked you to sponsor him?

Let's say you belong to a bike club. What if another bike club member asked you to sponsor him? You don't know him, but he has similar interests to you—you are both active in the bike club.

How do these different relationships affect your tendency to do what others want you to do?

Fenna Krienen (Krienen 2010) conducted research on whether the brain reacts differently based on whether we know people or agree with them. Krienen and team found that when people thought about friends or relatives—people they knew well—the medial prefrontal cortex (MPFC) was active, even if it was a relative they didn't have much in common with. The MPFC is the part of the brain that is active in perceiving value and regulating social behavior. When people thought about others that they didn't know, but did have common interests with (were similar to), the MPFC was not active.

It seems that our brains react in a special way to people we know. People are more likely to do stuff if they know the person who is asking them, regardless of whether they have differences of opinion with the person.

Similarity Builds Rapport

We find it easier to like those we feel are similar to us, or those whom we believe share our background or values. It can even boil down to clothes. We like people who dress as we do.

We make these decisions very quickly, and the decisions are not immediately conscious. In the book *Strangers to Ourselves: Discovering the Adaptive Unconscious* (Wilson 2004), Timothy Wilson talks about the processing that happens in our unconscious, "old" brain. It's called the "old" brain because it evolved long ago. We share the old brain with mammals, and even reptiles and amphibians.

The old brain monitors the environment and looks for danger. It's not immediately connected to the part of the brain that is conscious and thinking (the "new" brain—called "new" because it evolved most recently). So there's a lot of processing and decision making that occurs that you're not even aware of.

"Sizing up" other people is one of those types of processing. The old brain is making sure you're safe, and it does that by quickly sizing up the situation, the environment, and the other people nearby. The old brain then decides whether you should flee the situation, have sex, or eat something! It sounds crude and primitive, but that's what the old brain is: crude and primitive.

There's a lot of information to process, and all that processing is done in a split second. To process that quickly, the old brain takes a lot of shortcuts and makes broad generalizations.

Let's go back to the fundraising scenario from the beginning of this section. The old brain will size up the speaker. If the speaker is similar to you, then the decision (remember, all unconsciously) will be that you are safe and don't have to flee. This will also send signals to the midbrain (where emotions are processed) that this is someone you can trust.

After your old brain has finished its processing, you will either still be listening to the speaker or you will have disregarded him or her, left the room, or started daydreaming.

People are More Likely to Listen to and Be Persuaded by Attractive People

There has been a lot of research about the advantages given to people who are judged as attractive. Attractive people are seen to be smarter and more generous, kinder, and more intelligent. We make these judgments without realizing that we're doing so. Attractive people are more likely to get help when they are in need. And they are more persuasive in changing opinions.

The old brain is constantly evaluating the attractiveness of whomever you're interacting with. If your old brain decides that the person you're talking to is attractive, then you pay more attention to the person and you're more persuaded by what he or she is saying.

A MATHEMATICAL FORMULA FOR ATTRACTIVENESS?

In a study by Hatice Gunes (Gunes 2006), researchers took many different measurements of human faces. For example, they measured the distance from the top of the eyes to the bottom of the chin, the distance from the top of the eyes to the bottom of the nostrils, and so on. They compared these measurements to people's ratings of who was attractive. They found that most people agreed on who was attractive, and that those rated as attractive had certain proportions to their facial structures.

Although attractiveness is affected by cultural and surface norms, such as clothing and hair, there does seem to be a mathematical basis to decisions about who is attractive and that basis seems to hold true across cultures.

Michael Efran and E.W.J. Patterson (Efran 1974) analyzed elections in Canada and found that attractive candidates received more than two and a half times as many votes despite the fact that 73 percent of voters said that attractiveness did not influence their vote.

In a study by Shelly Chaiken (Chaiken 1979), attractive people were more likely to get other people to agree with them after giving a presentation. But part of the reason was that attractive people are more confident. Attractiveness and confidence are connected. The more attractive a person is, the more confident their presentation or conversation or request for action will be, and hence, the more likely it is that someone will agree to do what they want them to do.

If you combine an attractive person with a sexual implication, that's even more compelling. We talk about that in Chapter 6, "Instincts."

You're either "mathematically attractive" or you aren't, but whichever you are, you can use your clothing, posture, confidence, and facial expression to appear more attractive. Or you can get an attractive person to make a request for you.

Attractive people are more likely to get people to do stuff.

SNAG A CELEBRITY

Not everyone can get a celebrity to make appeals to donate for their cause, or can afford to hire a celebrity to help sell a product. If you can get the endorsement of a celebrity for your product or service, do it. People associate most celebrities with influence, attractiveness, wealth, and status.

STRATEGIES

Strategy 4: It matters who does the asking. It's most effective when the asking is done by a friend, someone attractive, or someone similar to those being asked.

Incur Debt

If you live in the US, then you probably know about the tradition of holiday cards. People send brightly colored cards with best wishes for the holidays and the new year. One year I sent a holiday card to several of the consultants that I worked with. One of them had only been with the company a few months—I'll call him John (not his real name). I didn't know him very well, but I sent a card anyway. He sent me one back. Shortly after that he left the company. I never saw him again.

John continued, however, to send me a holiday card and details of his family, including pictures, for many years. And because he sent one to me, I felt compelled to reciprocate. Back and forth the cards and letters and photos came over more than 15 years, even though I had known this person only briefly through work.

When we give someone a gift, even a small one (like a holiday card) or do someone a favor, the other person feels indebted, and will want to give a gift or do a favor in return; possibly to be nice, but mainly to get rid of the feeling of indebtedness. This is a largely unconscious feeling, and it is quite strong. This is called reciprocity.

The theory is that this gift giving and favor swapping developed in human societies because it was useful in the survival of the species. If one person gave someone something (food, shelter, money, a gift, or a favor), that triggered the indebtedness. If the person who did the gifting found himself or herself in need of something in the future, he "called in" the favor. These arrangements encouraged cooperation between individuals in a group and that cooperation allowed the group to grow and support one another. According to J. R. Henrich (Henrich 2001), the principle of reciprocity occurs across all cultures.

You can use reciprocity to get people to do stuff. If you give people a gift, and then ask them to do something, they are more likely to agree.

HOW TO DOUBLE DONATIONS

Robert Cialdini (Cialdini 1975) researched reciprocity. He sent a mailing asking for donations for a veterans group in the US. The mailing generated an average response rate of 18 percent. But when the mailing campaign included address labels that were personalized to the recipient, the donations almost doubled to 35 percent. Even a small gift such as mailing labels triggered reciprocity.

The Sizes of the Gifts Don't Have to Match

If you take me out to a nice dinner and pay the bill, then I will feel indebted to you. I will want to relieve the indebtedness. But I don't have to invite you to dinner at the same place and pay the bill. I don't have to take you to a place that is just as, or even more, expensive. The size of the gift can vary as long as I do you a favor or give you a gift.

Oftentimes it's enough if the reciprocating person does something as small as buying a cup of coffee. Money doesn't even have to be involved. I could relieve the debt by running an errand for you.

Reciprocity Is in the Eyes of the Debtor

The feeling that there is a debt owed comes from the person who owes the debt. If you do a favor for me you feel just fine. I'm the one who feels anxious and wants to relieve the debt. Whether the size of the gift or favor is large enough to relieve the debt is based on the point of view of the person who owes the debt.

 STRATEGIES

Strategy 5: Before you try to get people to do stuff, do something for them so they feel the need to reciprocate.

Get People to Say No

Why would I want someone to say "no" to what I want them to do? Imagine that you're giving a presentation to your local school board. You're part of a group of parents that would like to get new playground equipment. The parent group has selected you to approach the school board and ask for $2,000 (USD) for the playground equipment project.

At the meeting where you're making the presentation and request, you shock the rest of the parent group by asking for $5,000, not $2,000. The members of the school board say, "No, no, we can't possibly spend that much money for playground equipment." You look disappointed and then say, "Oh, well, we do have a reduced plan for $2,000." They ask to see the reduced plan, and you walk out of the meeting with the $2,000 project approved.

What just happened is called concession. When the school board said no, and you accepted that no, the no acted as a gift to the school board. As a result, they had now incurred a debt to you. When you offered the reduced plan for $2,000, they could relieve the indebtedness by saying "yes" to the reduced amount.

This tactic is sometimes called "rejection then retreat." The initiator asks a favor that is well above what most people would agree to. After the refusal, the initiator then asks for another favor that is more reasonable and receives exactly what he or she wanted in the first place.

Concession Builds Commitment, Too

In his research, Robert Cialdini (Cialdini 2006) stopped people on the street and asked them to chaperone a group of troubled youth on a one-day trip to the zoo. Only 17 percent of people said yes.

Some of the time he first asked people to spend two hours a week as a counselor for the youth for a minimum of two years (a larger request). In that case everyone said no. But if he then asked them to chaperone a group of troubled youth on a one-day trip to the zoo, 50 percent agreed. That's nearly three times the 17 percent who agreed when they were only asked to chaperone. That's concession working.

Cialdini also found an interesting side effect. Eighty-five percent of the people in the concession group actually showed up, compared with only 50 percent of the group that did not go through the concession process. Concession not only got people to say yes, it also increased their commitment to the action.

THE DIFFERENCE BETWEEN THE REQUEST SIZES MATTERS

For concession to have an effect, the first offer has to be beyond what people will normally agree to, but still has to be considered reasonable. If the first offer is totally outlandish, the retreat (second) request won't work. In addition, the retreat offer has to be seen as "fair."

 STRATEGIES
Strategy 6: Ask for more than you really want. When you get turned down, ask for what you really want.

Use Imitation

If you put your face right in front of a baby and stick out your tongue, the baby will stick out his or her tongue too. This happens from a very young age (even as young as one month old). So? What does this have to do with getting people to do stuff? It's an example of our built-in, wired-into-our-brain capacity for imitation. Recent research on the brain shows how our imitative behavior happens.

In the front of the brain there's an area called the premotor cortex (motor, as in movement). This is not the part of the brain where you actually send out the signals that make you move. *That* part of the brain is the primary motor cortex. The premotor cortex makes *plans* to move.

Let's say you're holding an ice cream cone. You notice that the ice cream is dripping, and you think that maybe you should lick off the dripping part before it drips on your shirt. If you were hooked up to an fMRI machine, you'd see the premotor cortex light up while you were thinking about licking off the dripping cone, and then you'd see the primary motor cortex light as you moved your arm.

Now here comes the interesting part. Let's say it's not you that has the dripping ice cream cone. It's your friend. You're watching your friend's cone start to drip. If you watch your friend lift his arm and lick the dripping cone, a subset of the same neurons also fires in your brain in the premotor cortex. Just watching other people take an action causes some of the same neurons to fire as if you were actually taking the action yourself. This subset of neurons has been dubbed "mirror neurons."

The latest theories are that these mirror neurons are also the way we empathize with others. We are literally experiencing what others are experiencing through these mirror neurons, and that allows us to deeply, and literally, understand how others feel.

MODEL THE BEHAVIOR

One way, then, to get people to do stuff is to model the behavior. Someone told me how she would get her roommates to clean up the apartment: while having a conversation about something, she would start to clean up the apartment. Then she would start handing things to the roommate and indicate with a hand gesture or movement of her head that the roommate should put things away. The roommate would start to imitate her behavior and would end up cleaning up too.

STRATEGIES

Strategy 7: To get people to do something, make sure you're doing it first (because they will imitate you).

Mimic Body Language to Build Rapport

Watch two people talking. If you observe them closely you'll see that over time they start to imitate each other's body language. If one leans in, the other leans in. If one touches his face, the other person touches his face.

Tanya Chartrand (Chartrand 1999) had people sit down and talk with someone (a "confederate" who was actually part of the experiment, but the participants didn't know that). The confederate would make various gestures and movements in a planned way. Some confederates were told to smile a lot, others to touch their face, and others to jiggle their foot. The participants in the study would start to (unconsciously) imitate their confederates. Some behaviors increased more than others. Face touching increased by 20 percent but foot jiggling increased by 50 percent.

In another experiment Chartrand and her colleague John Bargh put participants in two groups:

- In one group, the confederate imitated the participant's movements.
- In the second group, the confederate did not imitate the participant.

After the conversation, the participants were asked how much they liked their confederate, and how well they thought the interaction had gone. The group where the confederate had imitated the participant gave the confederate and the interaction higher ratings than the group where the confederate had not imitated the participant.

Earlier in this chapter we said that if people feel they are similar to you, then they're more likely to be persuaded by you. If you're trying to get people to do something, mimic their body position and facial expressions as you talk to them. This will build rapport, make them feel that you're similar to them, and make them like you.

All these things will make it more likely that they'll do whatever it is that you want them to do.

STRATEGIES

Strategy 8: To build rapport, imitate others' body positions and gestures. This builds connectedness and makes them more likely to do what you ask of them.

People Will Imitate Your Feelings

Not only do your facial expressions and body language communicate information and affect how people react to you and your message, they may also cause other people to feel a certain way.

Have you ever watched someone else watching a movie or a TV show? Or watched someone listening to a friend tell a story? If you do, you'll see that the person who's watching mirrors the expressions and even body language of the person they're listening to or watching.

EMOTIONS ARE CONTAGIOUS

Emotions can spread through a group the same way a cold or the flu can, and a lot faster. Earlier in this chapter we talked about social validation—the idea that people look to others to decide what to do—and imitation and mimicry. If you combine social validation, imitation, and mimicry, you start to understand how emotions can be noticed, identified, and reproduced in other people.

Elaine Hatfield researched the idea of "emotional contagion" (Hatfield 1993). When a message or idea is emotional and it gains momentum within a group, then emotional contagion happens and an idea, feeling, or action goes viral.

People imitate what they see. If you're smiling, those around you will tend to smile. If you're energetic, they'll be energetic too. This means that when you make your pitch to get someone to do something, you need to pay attention to your body language, your voice, and your passion for the topic. Whatever your thoughts and feelings are, they're communicated through your words, tone of voice, and body language, and picked up and felt by the person you're talking to.

STRATEGIES

Strategy 9: To get people to do something, show that you're passionate about what you're asking them to do.

Go Viral

Many of the topics in this book are about getting one or a few people to do stuff, understanding what motivates an individual, and having time to work with someone in particular to get them to do something.

But what if you want lots of people, like hundreds or thousands or more, to do stuff? Is there any psychology research that can tell you how to get lots of people to do stuff?

The answer is yes!

One way to get a lot of people to do something is for your idea or message to "go viral." The Urban Dictionary defines this as "an image, video, or link that spreads rapidly through a population by being frequently shared with a number of individuals." When something goes viral, it gains the power of social validation, which we covered earlier in this chapter, behind it. When your idea or message circulates virally, other people will want to join in and do what everyone else is doing.

In *The Dragonfly Effect*, Jennifer Aaker and Andy Smith tell the story of a young man named Sameer who needed a bone marrow transplant. He didn't have a donor who matched, so his friends and colleagues went to work getting out the message. Their goal was to get 20,000 people from India to register in the bone marrow registry in three weeks. That's the number they had calculated they would need to get a match. They used technology to get the word out. And they reached their goal.

Why do some ideas and some calls to action go viral and others don't?

What Goes Viral?

Jonah Berger (Berger 2011) analyzed articles from the *New York Times* to see which ones went viral and which did not. He looked at over 7,000 articles over a three-month period.

His conclusion was that the most important element of a message going viral is that it elicits a strong emotional reaction. At the top of the list are messages that elicit strong positive emotions, for example, awe, but right behind those are messages that elicit strong negative emotions such as anger or anxiety.

In *The Dragonfly Effect,* Aaker and Smith added to this analysis. In addition to emotions, messages go viral and get people to take action if they communicate the passion and commitment of the person and organization behind the message, and if they include a story (see Chapter 4, "The Power of Stories," for more on the impact of stories).

STRATEGIES

Strategy 10: To make something go viral, use strong emotional content, passion, and a good story to communicate the idea or the call to action.

The Science of Bonding

What do members of a marching band, fans cheering at a high school football game, and people at church have in common? They're all engaging in "synchronous" activity.

Anthropologists have long been interested in rituals in certain cultures, such as drumming, dancing, and singing. Scott Wiltermuth and Chip Heath (Wiltermuth 2009) conducted a series of studies to see whether, and how, synchronous behavior affects how people cooperate. They tested out combinations of walking in step, not walking in step, singing together, and other movements with groups of participants.

What they found was that people who engaged in synchronous activities were more cooperative in completing subsequent tasks, and more willing to make personal sacrifices to benefit the group.

Synchronous activities are actions you take together with others, where everyone is doing the same thing at the same time in physical proximity to one another. Dancing, tai chi, yoga, singing, clapping, and chanting in time with one another are all examples of synchronous activity.

THE MAGIC BONDING HORMONE

So why exactly do people bond when they do something together like laughing, clapping, or singing?

The bonding happens because of a hormone called oxytocin. All people release oxytocin at certain times, although it's more active in women. The most well-known cause of oxytocin release is childbirth and nursing. But oxytocin is also related to emotions. When oxytocin is released after a woman gives birth, it is responsible for feelings of maternal bonding. But oxytocin is active outside childbirth.

In *The Moral Molecule,* Paul Zak (Zak 2012) discusses the research showing that when people bond through group activity, oxytocin levels are elevated. This explains why doing group activities bonds the group.

Whenever oxytocin is released, we feel love, tenderness, empathy, and trust. We feel a sense of belonging and connectedness. People who are incapable of releasing oxytocin into their systems have a tendency to become sociopathic, psychopathic, or narcissistic.

When you hug someone or stroke a cat or dog, your body releases oxytocin. In fact, research shows that not only does your oxytocin level go up, but so does the dog's.

You could also think of oxytocin as the tribal hormone. Some research shows that oxytocin is related to a feeling of connectedness to one's group or tribe, and suspicion of "others" outside the group or tribe.

Wiltermuth and Heath's research also showed that you don't have to feel good about the group, or the group activity, in order to be more cooperative. Just the act of doing the synchronous activity seems to strengthen social attachment among the group members.

Laughter Bonds People

How many times a day do you hear someone laugh? Laughter is ubiquitous, so we don't even stop to think about what it is and why people do it.

There isn't as much research on laughter as you would think. But a few people have spent time researching it. Robert Provine (Provine 2001) is one of the few neuroscientists who has studied laughter. He concluded that laughter is an instinctual (not learned) behavior that creates social bonding.

THE LOWDOWN ON LAUGHTER

Robert Provine has spent many hours observing when and why people laugh. He and his team observed 1,200 people spontaneously laughing, in different locations. They took notes on gender, situation, speaker, listener, and context. Here's a summary of what they found:

- Laughter is universal: All humans in all cultures laugh.
- Laughter is unconscious: You can't actually laugh on command—it will be fake laughter if you try to.
- Laughter is for social communication: We rarely laugh when we're alone. We laugh 30 times more often when we're with others.
- Laughter is contagious: We smile and then start laughing as we hear others laugh.
- Laughter appears early in babies, at about 4 months old.
- Laughter is not about humor: Provine studied over 2,000 cases of naturally occurring laughter and most of it did not happen as a result of "humor" such as telling jokes. Most laughter followed statements such as "Hey, John, where ya been?" or "Here comes Mary" or "How did you do on the test?" Laughter after these types of statements bonds people together socially. Only 20 percent of laughter is from jokes.
- We rarely laugh in the middle of a sentence. It's usually at the end.
- Most laughing is done by the person who is speaking, not the person who is listening. The person who is speaking laughs twice as much.
- Women laugh more than twice as much as men.
- Laughter denotes social status. The higher you are in the hierarchy of a group, the *less* you will laugh.

 STRATEGIES

Strategy 11: To get people to do something, first bond them together as a group with some kind of laughter or synchronous behavior.

DO PEOPLE NEED SYNCHRONOUS ACTIVITY TO BE HAPPY?

In his article "Hive Psychology, Happiness, and Public Policy," Jonathan Haidt (Haidt 2008) goes so far as to say that because synchronous activity promotes bonding, it therefore helps the survival of the group. He believes that there's a certain type of happiness that humans can get only by engaging in synchronous activity. For example, many people like the experience of playing in a band or orchestra, singing in a choir, or even attending church. These are all synchronous activities.

How to Get People to Trust You

If people trust you, then they'll be more likely to do what you want them to do. But how do you get them to trust you?

It turns out that there's a very easy way to get people to trust you. All you have to do is trigger the release of oxytocin. OK, so how do you do that? The easiest way is to show that *you* trust *them*. When you do something that shows that you trust someone, they are much more likely to trust you back.

So how can you show people that you trust them? There are many ways. Here are some examples:

- Ask them to do an important task that you usually do yourself. And don't check up on them.
- Give someone the keys to your apartment and ask them to check on your pets or water your plants while you're gone.
- Let them borrow your car.
- Ask them to make a presentation at an important meeting.

When you take an action that shows that you trust someone, the person being trusted will release oxytocin. This, in turn, will make them more likely to trust you.

 STRATEGIES

Strategy 12: To get people to trust you, first show them that you trust them. When they trust you, they'll be more likely to do what you ask them to.

Syncing the Brains of Speakers with the Brains of Listeners

You want to make a request of someone you work with. You'd like him or her to work with you on a project, even though it means taking on extra work. So how should you approach them? What way will give you a better chance of them saying yes? Should you go visit their office in person? Or is it better to send a message?

Most communication experts would probably tell you to go talk to them. We all know that talking to someone in person is better than sending a message. If you're there in person you can get some laughter started, which will bond you. They can read your body language (which could be a good or bad thing depending on how well you communicate via body language). But it goes beyond that. It's also the sound of your voice that makes an important connection.

When you listen to someone talking, your brain starts working in sync with the speaker. Greg Stephens (Stephens 2010) put participants in his research study in an fMRI machine and had them listen to recordings of other people talking. He found that as someone is listening to someone else talk, the brain patterns of the two people start to couple, or mirror each other. There's a slight delay that corresponds to the time it takes for the communication to occur. Several different brain areas sync. He also had people listen to someone talk in a language they did not understand. In that case the brains did not sync up.

In Stephens's study, the more the brains were synced, the more the listener understood the ideas and message from the speaker. And by watching what parts of the brain were lighting up, Stephens could see that the parts of the brain that have to do with prediction and anticipation were active. The more active they were, the more successful was the communication.

The parts of the brain that have to do with social interaction were also synced. Areas involved in processing social information that are crucial for successful communication were active, including the capacity to discern the beliefs, desires, and goals of others.

Hearing someone's voice is much more effective than reading a message. If you want to get people to do stuff, they need to hear your voice, even if it's not in person.

STRATEGIES

Strategy 13: To get people to do something, sync your communication directly with their brains. They need to hear your voice.

When Competition Works and When It Doesn't

We take for granted that competition will motivate people to do stuff, and it can. But the research shows that there are some situations where competition is motivating and others where it isn't.

Competition Motivates Men, But It Does *Not* Motivate Women

Several research studies (Gneezy 2003) show gender differences in how boys and girls, or men and women, compete. Competition often increases performance for boys and men (as long as there aren't too many competitors—see the next section), but it doesn't always increase performance for girls and women. If women are competing against other women, or girls against girls, then there is sometimes an improvement in performance, although it's usually not large. And if women are competing against men, or girls against boys, then the women and girls often show no improvement in performance using competition.

Fewer Competitors Equals More Competitive Behaviors

Did you take a standardized test like the SAT or ACT to get into college? How many people were in the room when you took the test? What does it matter? Research by Stephen Garcia and Avishalom Tor (Garcia 2009) shows that it may matter a lot.

Garcia and Tor first compared SAT scores for locations that had many people in the room taking the test versus locations that had smaller numbers. They adjusted the scores to control for differences in regional education budgets and other factors. Students who took the SAT test in a room with fewer people scored higher.

Garcia and Tor hypothesized that when there are only a few competitors, we (perhaps unconsciously) feel that we can come out on top, and so we try harder. And, the theory goes, when there are more people, it's harder to assess where we stand and therefore we're less motivated to try to come out on top. They called this the *N*-effect, with *N* equaling number, as in formulas.

Competing against 10 Competitors vs. Competing against 100

Garcia and Tor next decided to test their theory in the lab. They asked students to complete a short quiz, and told them to complete it as quickly and accurately as possible. They were told that the top 20 percent would receive $5.

Group A was told that they were competing against 10 other students. Group B was told that they were competing against 100 other students. Participants in Group A completed the quiz significantly faster than those in Group B.

The interesting thing is that there was no one actually in the room with them. They were just told that other people were taking the test.

If you want men to do stuff, then try setting up a competition with a small number of other men. If you want women to do stuff, avoid setting them in competition at all—and don't have them compete with men.

STRATEGIES

Strategy 14: Use competition only with a small number (fewer than 10) of competitors.

Strategy 15: Don't mix men and women in a competition.

People Follow Leaders

Research in psychology over the last 15 years has revealed that people process information unconsciously and make very quick (a second or less) unconscious decisions about people.

If you're going to get people to do stuff, you need them to unconsciously assign you leader status. There are many things you can do to make sure that you're seen as a leader.

People Follow a Leader They Identify With

In the early sixties, Stanley Milgram (Milgram 1963) performed experiments on the psychology of obedience. Participants in the study thought they were engaged in an experiment on learning and punishments. They were asked to administer shocks to someone in another room if they answered questions incorrectly. In fact the person in the other room was part of the experiment, and wasn't receiving shocks at all.

Every time the "learner" answered a question incorrectly, the participants were asked to increase the level of shock voltage. The participants couldn't

MILGRAM'S ETHICS FIRESTORM

Stanley Milgram's experiments set off a firestorm about the ethics of working with participants. Years later some of the participants in the Milgram studies reported long-term psychological damage ("What kind of person am I that I would shock people?"). Since then psychology experiments in most countries have to adhere to guidelines to prevent harm to the participants.

see the "learner" but they could hear them making noise every time they received a shock. As the voltage was increased the "learner" made more and more noise, eventually shouting things like "Stop, please stop!" Eventually, at the highest voltage levels the "learner" was silent, as though they had passed out or were unconscious.

Milgram was trying to understand how far people would go against their own moral code to inflict pain on another person if an authority figure told them they had to. Before the experiments started, Milgram asked colleagues, grad students, and psychology majors at Yale (where the study was conducted) to estimate how many people would up the voltage the maximum amount (30 steps up from where it started) if an authority figure in a lab coat told them to do so. The estimate was one to two percent. In the experiment, however, two thirds of the subjects went to the maximum, even with the (pretend) subject in the other room shouting, "Please stop!"

Since the 1960s most psychologists refer to this study as an example of obedience to authority. But in 2012 Alexander Haslam and Stephen Reicher reanalyzed the data from the study. They argue that it's more about identification with a group than obedience to authority. People who identified with the learner in the experiment refused to give the shocks. Those who identified with the experimenter were more likely to give the shocks (Haslam 2012).

When we identify with a group, we are much more willing to follow the beliefs and actions of the group and we are then much more likely to follow the leader of a group. If you combine a dominant leader with identification with a group, then it's much easier to get people to do stuff.

Before you ask people to do something, engage them in an activity that makes them feel that they identify with the group you are in or that you represent. For example, you might use one of the bonding techniques we covered earlier in this chapter. Once the group is bonded, and they feel like a group, then establish yourself as the leader, using one or more of the techniques that follow.

Convey Leadership with Your Body Language

Hannah is going to talk to her team about getting them to follow a new work process. She calls the group together for a meeting. It's important that they get behind the new ideas, and she's nervous about how the team will react.

As the meeting starts she is standing behind a table, her shoulders are slumped forward, and she's not making eye contact. When she starts talking she glances up briefly, then looks at her laptop and crosses her arms. She may not realize it, but she's sending the message that she's very nervous. She is not inspiring confidence.

The way you walk and stand, your facial expressions, and your eye contact, or lack of it, communicate if you are nervous, confident, excited, and more. Decide what impression you want to convey, and then think about how your body language is conveying it. People *want* a strong leader. If your body language exudes confidence, then your audience will be inspired to follow you.

TAKE TIME TO "SET" YOUR BODY

Before you ask someone to do something, "set" your body. Face the person or people you are talking to, stand firmly with even weight on both feet, look at the person or people, make eye contact, take a breath, and then begin. It will seem like too much time has passed without talking, but that's not how it appears from the other person's point of view.

In addition to an initial first impression, people continue to unconsciously interpret and react to your body positions throughout your conversation.

Be Aware of the Angle of Your Stance

To convey authority and confidence, face people directly. To convey collaboration, stand at an angle to the person you're talking to. Don't allow any barriers between you and the people you're talking to. People need to see your body in order to trust you. Showing your body conveys trust, confidence, and authority.

Consider the Position of Your Head

When you're talking one-on-one with someone, tilting your head conveys that you're interested in them or what they're saying, but it can also be a sign of submission. If you want to convey authority and confidence, avoid tilting your head.

Stand with Balanced Weight

Standing firmly with your weight evenly balanced on both legs says you are sure and confident. Putting weight on only one foot, or leaning against something like a table or chair undermines your confidence and authority.

Don't Fidget

Not too long ago I spoke at a conference with a line-up of great presenters. One man whom I had been looking forward to hearing got up to speak. He is well known in his field, but I had never attended one of his live presentations.

His talk was very good, but I couldn't concentrate on it because throughout the entire talk he made a small movement over and over. He would step forward with one foot, then step back with the other, like a little dance, over and over. It was a form of fidgeting, and it was very distracting.

Fidgeting like this takes many forms. Some people rattle keys in their pocket, or tap their foot or fingers. Fidgeting conveys that you're nervous, bored, or impatient. A fidgeter is not a leader.

Dealing with Nervousness

There will be times when you'll be nervous asking people to do stuff. Being a little nervous can be a good thing, since it will keep you alert and make you excited. But being too nervous is a bad thing. Nervousness is contagious. If you're nervous it will hurt your confidence and position as a leader.

Muscles and emotions are a two-way feedback loop. When you feel emotions, your body shows those feelings. For example, if you feel sad, your shoulders slump, you don't stand up straight, and your mouth muscles move downward. But did you realize that the opposite is true? If you stand up straight and smile, your mood will improve. Research by Pablo Briñol (Briñol 2009), shows that when people take postures of confidence, they then actually feel more confident.

Before you begin a conversation where you're asking people to do stuff, go to another room, or into the hallway, and work on your body position. Breathe deeply and stand straight with your head straight.

If you take on this confident body posture, you'll feel more confident.

STRATEGIES

Strategy 16: People are more likely to do what you want them to do when they consider you a leader. To be seen as a leader, you must show confidence via your body posture and stance.

What Are You Saying with Your Hands?

Have you ever watched a video of yourself in conversation with someone else? If someone were able to video record you while you're engaged in a natural conversation, what would your hand gestures "say"?

Watch people talking and gesturing. Some people use hand gestures that are a good match to what they are saying. Others make overly large gestures that can be distracting, and others don't use their hands much at all. No matter which camp you fall into, it's important to pay attention to your hand gestures and perhaps practice some new ones.

Using no hand gestures at all conveys a lack of interest. Make sure the people you're talking to can see your hands. If they can't see your hands at all, it will be hard for them to trust you.

- Hands open with palms up means you're asking for something from the audience.
- Hands open with palms at a 45-degree angle means you're being honest and open.
- Hands open with palms down means you're certain about what you're talking about.
- Hands at a 90-degree angle and fingers together means you have confidence and expertise about what you're saying.
- Hands touching your face, hair, or neck make you look nervous or tentative, as do hands grasped together in front of you.
- Standing with your hands on your hips indicates aggressiveness. There are times when this might be appropriate, for example in a negotiation, but think twice before using it.

▶ **NOTE** My favorite book on body language is *The Silent Language of Leaders: How Body Language Can Help—or Hurt—How You Lead* by Carol Kinsey Goman (Jossey-Bass, 2011).

HAND GESTURES CAN HAVE CULTURAL MEANINGS

A few years ago I was a speaker at a conference in Lisbon, Portugal. It was my first time there, and I became instantly enamored of the special custard pastries that Lisbon is known for.

One morning I went into a bakery and ordered two of the pastries. I did so by holding up two fingers, similar to the "victory" or "peace" gesture in the US. The person behind the counter at the bakery proceeded to put three pastries in a box. I later learned that the gesture for two would have been to raise my thumb and index finger. Even though my thumb wasn't showing, the person behind the counter thought I was signaling for three.

I was lucky that I didn't get into more trouble than an extra pastry. Many hand gestures are not universal. If you're talking to people from another country or culture that you're unfamiliar with, do some research to find out which gestures might be misunderstood, not understood at all, or offensive.

It's OK to use hand gestures that are larger than the outlines of your body now and then to indicate something specific. For example, if you're talking about a new, large change in your organization, then your hands might extend outward beyond your body. But if all of your gestures are that large you'll be seen as chaotic or out of control.

 STRATEGIES

Strategy 17: To be persuasive, your hand gestures must match what you're saying.

Your Face and Eyes Are Talking, Too

There's a special part of the brain that pays attention to faces. It's called the fusiform facial area (FFA). The FFA is in the emotional part of the brain. Your face conveys important emotional information to the people you're in conversation with. Your face and eye movements affect your message.

Unconscious Facial Expressions

Have you ever watched newscasters closely on TV? They always have a slight smile, even when they're announcing bad or sad news. This is something that does not come naturally, and has to be practiced until it's somewhat automatic.

Try this exercise: prepare a few sentences of a conversation you may have with someone you're asking to do something. Memorize the words so you don't have to look at your notes to say the few sentences. Now stand in front of a mirror and say the sentences as though you're in conversation with the person. Unless you were telling a funny story, chances are your expression in the mirror was quite somber.

It's easy to forget that our faces show many expressions, and that we might not be aware of them. When you're asking people to do stuff, you might be thinking hard and therefore tend to frown, or perhaps you get nervous and forget what you were going to say and look panicked. The person you're talking to is going to react to your facial expressions.

Some facial expressions and eye movements to watch out for are

- Blinking a lot: This can be a sign of nervousness. Blinking can communicate that you are uncomfortable. It can also be interpreted as a sign of attraction to the person you're looking at.
- Direct eye gaze: Looking directly at someone during a conversation conveys that you're interested and paying attention. Staring for too long at one person, however, indicates that you're threatening them.
- Frequent eye shifting: Communicates that you're nervous or lying.
- Chewing on your bottom lip or biting your lips: Conveys worry, insecurity, and fear.
- Wide eyes and slightly raised eyebrows: Signifies alertness and interest.

STRATEGIES

Strategy 18: You'll be more persuasive when you look directly at a person and use a slight smile.

You Communicate Meaning with Your Tone of Voice

If you've ever traveled in a country where you did not speak the language and eavesdropped on a conversation, you might have been surprised to find yourself following along and picking up the feeling of the conversation even though you didn't understand any of the words. The field of paralinguistics studies vocal communication that is separate from the words that are spoken.

Think about this for a minute. You can say "This new team configuration will work out great" in many different ways. You can say it with a lot of enthusiasm, or with sarcasm, or with boredom. The way you say the sentence conveys as much meaning or more than the words themselves. Here are some things to think about:

- Vary the pitch and volume of your voice, based on the meaning of what you're saying. If you talk at the same pitch and volume all the time, you'll sound boring and appear to lack emotion or passion for your topic.
- Match your paralinguistics with your message. If you're excited or passionate about an idea, convey that passion by speaking a little louder, a little faster, and with more variety in your pitch.
- Speak loudly enough for your audience to hear you. Being too soft spoken conveys timidity or nervousness.
- Pronounce all of your words. Watch out especially for the endings of words and the endings of sentences. These are the places that people tend to cut off. Articulating well conveys confidence and authority.
- Think about using pauses. If you get nervous, you'll tend to talk faster and faster with few pauses. Pause before and after you make an important statement or ask a question. Your silence can be as important as your words.

 STRATEGIES
Strategy 19: To excite someone to do something, communicate with energy and enthusiasm.

Clothes Do Make You

You've probably heard the phrases "clothes make the man" or "dress for success." Research actually backs up these two sayings.

Monroe Lefkowitz, Robert Blake, and Jane Mouton (1955) had an experimenter cross the street against the traffic light in a city. When he was dressed in a suit, three and a half times as many people followed him as when he wore a work shirt and trousers. Business suits convey authority.

In a study by Leonard Bickman (Bickman 1974) the experimenter stopped a person on the street, pointed to an accomplice 50 feet away, and said, "You see that guy over there by the meter? He's overparked but doesn't have any change. Give him a dime!" and then would leave.

The "guy over there" was part of the experiment. If the person giving the command had a uniform on, for example, a guard uniform, then most people complied with the instruction to give money for the parking meter. If he was dressed in regular street clothes, then the compliance was less than half.

You'll have to decide whether you're dressing for authority or similarity. The guideline for how to dress in a position of authority is to dress at least one notch above the people you're talking to. If it's more important to be seen as "one of the group," then dress similarly to those you're talking to.

STRATEGIES

Strategy 20: To get people to do stuff, you must either dress like them to make use of similarity or dress a notch above them to make use of authority.

How to Become the Leader in a Few Seconds

Cameron Anderson and Gavin Kilduff (Anderson 2009) researched group decision making. They formed groups of four students each and had them solve math problems from the GMAT (a standardized test for admission to graduate business school programs). Using standardized math problems allowed the researchers to evaluate how well the group solved the problems they were given. It also allowed them to compare each member's competence by looking at their previous SAT math scores from their undergraduate admission to college.

The researchers videotaped the group conversations during the problem-solving session and reviewed them later to decide who was the leader of each group. They had multiple sets of observers view the videos to see if there was consensus about who the leaders were. They also asked the people in the groups to identify the leader of their group. Everyone agreed on who the leader was in each group.

Anderson and Kilduff were interested in why the leaders became the leaders. Before the groups started, everyone filled out a questionnaire to measure their level of dominance. As you might imagine, the leaders all scored high on the dominance measure. But that still doesn't suggest how they became leaders. Did they have the best math SAT scores? (No.) Did they bully everyone else into letting them be the leader? (No.)

The answer surprised the researchers: The leaders spoke first. For 94 percent of the problems, the group's final answer was the first answer that was proposed, and the people with the dominant personalities always spoke first.

People will listen to the leader and be more likely to do what the leader suggests. If you want to be the leader, and if you want people to do stuff, make sure you speak first.

 STRATEGIES

Strategy 21: Talk first and you will be seen as the leader. When you're the leader, you'll be more likely to get people to do stuff.

3

Habits

WHETHER YOU REALIZE it or not, a lot of your daily behavior is composed of habits. These are automatic behaviors that you do without thinking. You do them the same way every day.

Your conscious experiences of trying to change your own habits may not be positive. Maybe you've tried to quit smoking, or tried to exercise more. Has it seemed hard to get a new habit started, or get rid of an old one? If so, you might be wondering why I'd suggest working with habits as a way to get people to do stuff.

Habits *can* be hard to start and hard to change, but if you understand the science around how habits are formed, you'll see that there are some fairly simple things you can do that make habits very easy to form and even relatively easy to change.

In fact, there are two reasons why understanding and working with habits is valuable if you want to get people to do stuff:

1. Since habits are so automatic, if you can get people to create a new habit doing what you want them to do, it's likely that they'll automatically repeat that behavior for a long time without you needing to do anything else.
2. If you know someone's current habits, you can attach a new habit to one of those existing habits.

The Science of Habits

In *The Power of Habit* (Duhigg 2012), Charles Duhigg covers the latest science about habits. He explains how habits are formed and he connects cues, routines, and rewards.

When someone has formed a habit, there's a cue that triggers the habit, then there's the routine of the habit that is automatically carried out, and that's followed by a reward that has to do with the purpose of the habit.

The reward strengthens the habit and sets it up to happen again the next time the cue appears:

Cue → Routine → Reward

In his book, Duhigg actually draws this as a circle, since he connects the reward back to the cue.

Let's look at a simple example: most people have a set of routines or habits they go through when they wake up. Here's one of my morning routines:

- Brush my teeth.
- Use the Waterpik.
- Brush my hair.

I follow another routine early each day:

- Check my email.
- Check my calendar for the day.

And here's my breakfast routine:

- Put water on the stove for coffee (I use a cone where the coffee drips through instead of a coffee machine).
- Start an egg cooking.
- Start some toast.

Your routine may be different, but like all of us, you probably have routines for hundreds of things you do during the day:

- How you leave the house for work
- How you drive or walk to work
- How you settle in when you get to work
- How you clean your house or apartment
- How you do laundry
- How you shop for a gift for a relative
- How and where you exercise
- How you wash your hair
- How and when you water your houseplants
- When and where you take your dog for a walk
- What and when you feed your cat
- The rituals you have for putting your children to bed at night

Everyone has habits. For most people, most of the time, habits are created unconsciously and carried out automatically. Habits help us all to do the many things we need and want to do in our lives. Because we can carry out a habit without having to think about it, it frees up our thought processes to work on other things. It's a trick that our brains have evolved to make us more efficient.

 STRATEGIES

Strategy 22: To get people to do something automatically for a long time, get them to create a new habit or change an existing one.

How Habits Get Formed

If you understand how habits are formed, you can figure out how to get people to create new habits for the stuff you want them to do. Habits are *performed* automatically and unconsciously, but it turns out that we *create* them unconsciously too. We create most of our habits without realizing that we're doing it.

For example, let's say one of your habits is to have a quick breakfast of toast and coffee at home every morning. One day your alarm doesn't go off and you're late to work, so you shortcut or skip some of your regular habits. One of the routines you skip that day is breakfast—there just isn't time. On your way to work you stop at a café and pick up coffee and a pastry to take with you to work or even eat in the car.

A few days later the same thing happens—you really need to get a new alarm clock! But no problem, you'll stop at that same café and grab a coffee and pastry again.

The next day you wake up on time. You're not late this day, but you decide to skip breakfast at home, and instead stop at the café, and, you guessed it, get a coffee and a pastry. Now the new habit is set. What you did was disrupt the old habit. Remember Duhigg's habit loop:

Cue → Routine → Reward

Here's the old habit:

Come down the stairs → Make breakfast → Eat food

Now you have a new habit:

See café → Buy a coffee and a pastry → Eat food

If you want to get people to do stuff, and they have a habit already established, then you need to see if you can disrupt the old habit by creating a new one in its place. More specifically, in the case of habits that are formed unconsciously, you'll have to come up with a new Cue → Routine → Reward cycle to replace an existing Cue → Routine → Reward cycle.

Let's say you're a lawyer in a small law firm. You have a receptionist, Zoe, who always leaves her desk in disarray at the end of the day. It's her habit to work on things right up to the last minute of the workday.

When one of the paralegals, Jodi, leaves at the end of each day, she goes by Zoe's desk and says, "Bye, Zoe, see you tomorrow." That's when Zoe realizes that she's late to catch her train. At that point she goes flying out the door, leaving the work scattered all over.

Sometimes you have clients that come in early for meetings, before Zoe comes in to work to clean up the mess on her desk. You don't like people seeing her messy desk. You've thought about just moving her desk to an office with a door down the hall, but you really do need her by the front door, and she really needs line of sight to the door. This means that, conversely, anyone walking in the door has line of sight to her desk.

You've tried talking to her to get her to pay attention to the clock and spend some time cleaning up her desk before she leaves, but no matter how much you talk to her about it, it never seems to change.

Zoe has unconsciously created a habit loop:

Cue → Routine → Reward

Here's the habit:

Hear "Bye, Zoe" → Grab purse and coat and walk out door → Catch early train and get home before husband

You want to disrupt this habit and replace it with a new one. You want the new routine to be that she takes a few minutes and cleans up her desk before leaving:

Cue → Clean up desk → Reward

You need a new cue and a new reward.

Let's tackle the reward first.

Zoe has mentioned before that she doesn't get enough time with you to go over papers and decisions, so more time from you would be a reward. And she'd love to catch an earlier train, so that could be a reward. You could use just the first, or use them both together:

Cue → Clean up desk → 30 minutes to go over papers and so on with boss

Or

Cue → Clean up desk → 30 minutes to go over papers and so on with boss and leave 15 minutes early and catch an earlier train

Now you need to pick the cue. I suggest you start with yourself as the cue: About an hour before it's time for Zoe to leave, you say, "Zoe, is it 4:00

p.m.?" Zoe looks at her clock and says it is. "Why don't you straighten up your desk and then come in and we'll meet for 30 minutes to go over the papers you were asking me about." You might need to stand there while she cleans up her desk to make sure she does.

Next you spend the 30 minutes with her and then say, "That's enough for today. It's a little early, but your desk is all cleaned up, so why don't you leave a little early today and catch that earlier train."

Notice that Jodi hasn't had the chance to walk by and say "Bye, Zoe," because it isn't that late yet. This means you've disrupted the cue for the old habit.

Now you have the possibility of a new habit:

CUE   → *ROUTINE*   → *REWARD*

Boss says, → *Clean up* → *Spend 30 minutes with boss*
"Zoe, is it   *desk*   *clearing up annoying loose*
4:00 p.m.?"   *ends and get to leave a few*
                               minutes early

You took an old habit that was created unconsciously and replaced it with a conscious habit to start. The new habit will eventually become unconscious.

I suggest you run the loop as described above for about a week, and then switch out the cue. After a week of you saying "Zoe, is it 4:00 p.m.?" as the cue, try asking Zoe to set an alarm on her computer to go off at 4:00 p.m. each day, so the alarm becomes the cue. That way you don't have to always be the cue. But you should still check that the desk is clean for another week or two before finishing the loop with the meeting.

 STRATEGIES

Strategy 23: To get someone to create a new habit, figure out a cue and a reward.

How to Intentionally Engage the Unconscious

In the previous example, Zoe did not intentionally set out to change her own behavior. Because habits are carried out unconsciously, they're easy to create unconsciously.

But what about intentional habits? Can you get people to intentionally change a habit? You can, but you still have to engage the unconscious.

As we've seen, habits are carried out in a largely unconscious way. If we try to change a habit just with intentional, conscious thinking, it can be very difficult. We've all tried to change our own habits consciously and intentionally, and we've all had, at best, mixed results. We have to engage the unconscious in order for the habit to become automatic.

I'll use a personal story to show how this works. I'm a person who exercises moderately and regularly to stay healthy and relieve stress. But I can't say that I've ever been a person who actually enjoys exercise.

My friends and family have watched in amazement, however, as I recently started jogging. Not only have I taken up jogging, but I do it every other day, and I rarely miss a day. Not only do I jog every other day, I look forward to it—I relish the experience. What happened?

How did I go from being a person who exercises moderately because I know I should to a person who jogs for an hour several times a week and loves it? Is it because I set a New Year's resolution to get more exercise? Or did I say an affirmation like "I love jogging" a hundred times?

No, that's not how I did it. Most of it wasn't intentional.

I was visiting a friend in England, and she told me about an app she uses on her iPhone called "Couch to 5K." I thought it sounded interesting, so I downloaded the app and tried it out. I'm always looking for new technology gizmos to try out.

The app "talks" to you, telling you what to do. It starts very easy, mainly with a lot of walking and one-minute runs sprinkled throughout. A voice tells you exactly what to do and what's happening ("Start running," or "Slow down and walk," or "You have reached the halfway point").

In every exercise session there's an incremental increase in the amount of running versus walking, until, eventually, over the course of nine weeks, you're running 5K.

As you use the app you can see your progress on little charts and graphs. You can see how a session is progressing as you're in it, and you can see your progress overall.

The app makes use of three critical factors for getting people to create new, conscious habits. These are so critical that I call them "secrets":

- **Secret number 1** is that there must be incremental steps for the person to go through.
- **Secret number 2** is that once the person makes the decision to try it, there must be no other decisions to make. The individual must be taken

out of all the decision making. In the Couch to 5K app, starting the app is the only decision you make. Everything else (how long to run, how far to run, when to run versus when to walk, how long to warm up, how long to cool down) is decided by the app. The app decides everything for you.

- **Secret number 3** is that the person can see the progress toward the goal. It's especially important that people can see how far they have left to go (see Chapter 5, "Carrots and Sticks," for more on this concept).

If these three secrets are in place, then the habit becomes easy and effortless to initiate and to continue.

The Couch to 5K became a habit loop:

CUE   →   *ROUTINE*   →   *REWARD*

Voice says "Start → *Do everything* → *See my progress*
with a five-minute   *the voice says*   *on the chart*
warm-up walk"   *to do*

When I got to the end of the nine-week Couch to 5K program, I was sad. So I got the Couch to 10K app and started all over!

You can't actually create a habit for someone else—the person has to initiate the routine. But you can provide the initial cue. You can provide a framework, for example: an app, software, media, worksheets, and charts that break the routine into small steps. You can make the routine automatic so it's not necessary to make decisions. And you can provide that critical feedback on the individual's progress and what is left to finish the routine and reach the reward of the Cue → Routine → Reward habit cycle.

 STRATEGIES

Strategy 24: To encourage the creation of a habit, break the desired behavior into small steps.

Strategy 25: To get people to start a new habit, make it as easy as possible and eliminate all decision making except the decision to start the routine. All other steps should happen as automatically as possible.

Strategy 26: To get people to stick with the new routine and the new habit, show results and progress. Habits need lots of feedback on what is happening.

How to Create a New Habit in Less than a Week

I used to think that it was hard to create new habits. In fact, in some of my previous books I even included sections on how it takes a long time to create a new habit. I cited the Phillippa Lally (Lally 2010) study showing that the average amount of time it takes for people to form a habit is 66 days, with a range from 18 days for easier habits to 254 days for more complex habits.

But recently I had an experience that led me to the conclusion that habits don't have to take that long to create *if* you know how habits work and apply that knowledge. What changed my thinking? I signed up for B. J. Fogg's "3 Tiny Habits" program.

Fogg has made a career of understanding what persuades people. As of the writing of this book he has a simple experience you can try out through his website, tinyhabits.com.

You may think, like I did, that it's hard to create a new habit, but you can easily create three new habits in only a week. Try it. Go to the website and sign up. It takes about five to ten minutes to read the introductory information, about five minutes to decide on the three habits you're going to work on, and then only a minute or two per day to "practice" your habits.

Fogg gives you a week, but I found that in three days the habits were firmly established. As I write this it's been months and I'm still doing the three habits, every day, just like clockwork.

How is this possible? Doesn't this fly in the face of conventional wisdom about habits? The secret lies in anchoring. We know that existing habits are automatic and powerful. Why not use that? Why not piggyback on an existing habit and add to it to create a new habit?

First Fogg has you identify one small habit you'd like to create. He insists it has to be very small and very easy to do. One of the habits I picked was drinking half a glass of water first thing in the morning. I don't drink enough water, and I thought it would be a good habit to start with. The specific routine I was going to create was

Drink half a glass of water and refill the water glass

In order to make sure it would be easy, I kept a water glass in my bedroom.

The next step was to choose an anchor. An anchor is a cue that exists from a habit you already have. Every morning I wake up and take a medication for my thyroid deficiency. That's an established habit.

So that was my anchor for the new habit I was trying to create. For one week, every day after I took my medication, I would drink half a glass of water, then refill the water glass in the bathroom next door, and then put the water glass back on my bedroom table, ready for the next day.

EXISTING CUE	→	EXISITNG ROUTINE BECOMES THE NEW CUE	→	NEW ROUTINE
Get out of bed	→	Take medication becomes the new cue: Take medication	→	Drink half a glass of water and refill water glass

You anchor the new habit to an existing habit. It all becomes automatic and effortless. I now have three new habits that I didn't have before. It took me three days to establish them.

Fogg has you create three new habits. Drinking water was one. The other two I picked were

- Use a moisturizer on my hands and face each morning.
- Make a list of three things I want to accomplish that day, early in the day before I get distracted with work and forget to make the list.

I know these don't seem like life-changing habits, but the idea is to learn how to use anchoring and to find out how easy it is to create a new habit from an existing one.

In order to add these two new habits, I had to find existing habits to anchor them to. For the moisturizer I used brushing my teeth. I brush my teeth each morning, and that's an established habit that I don't have to think about.

EXISTING CUE	→	EXISITNG ROUTINE BECOMES THE NEW CUE	→	NEW ROUTINE
Wake up	→	Brush teeth becomes the new cue: Brush teeth	→	Put on moisturizer

For the list of three things I want to accomplish that day, I used the anchoring habit of checking my email. Every morning I check my email. That's a well-established habit I already have.

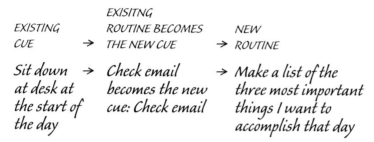

EXISTING CUE	→	EXISITNG ROUTINE BECOMES THE NEW CUE	→	NEW ROUTINE
Sit down at desk at the start of the day	→	*Check email becomes the new cue: Check email*	→	*Make a list of the three most important things I want to accomplish that day*

I was truly amazed. After years of thinking that it took months to learn new habits, I had easily added three new habits in a matter of days. Of course, these were easy and small habits, and that's the point. The habits that we do easily and effortlessly are small habits that we can anchor to existing, well-entrenched habits we already have.

Using Anchoring to Get Other People to Create New Habits

You can't make people create a habit if they don't want to, but you can certainly encourage someone to form a new habit through anchoring. You can analyze the situation and the existing habits and cues, and suggest

- What new habit to create
- What existing habit to anchor it to
- What the new cue and routine might be

Helping someone to create a new habit is a motivation driver that works best when you want people to change a specific behavior that is relatively small. If you have larger behaviors you want to change, or something less concrete (for example, changing an opinion rather than a specific behavior), then you'll need to use other drivers in this book.

But if you have small, concrete behaviors you want people to do, then habits and automatic behavior can deliver the behavior you're seeking.

 STRATEGIES

Strategy 27: To create a new habit, anchor it to an existing habit.

Strategy 28: Use new habit creation when you want people to do something that is relatively small, yet you want them to do it unconsciously and automatically.

4

The Power
of Stories

NO IDEA IN this book is more powerful than the idea of using stories to affect behavior. Everything we do is related to a story we have about who we are and how we relate to others. A lot of these stories are unconscious. Whether conscious or unconscious, our stories about ourselves deeply affect how we think and behave. If you can change someone's story, you can change behavior.

I remember a moment many years ago when I was having a series of crises. I was 30 years old. A long-term relationship had just ended in a difficult way. I had moved to a new city where I did not know anyone. I had started a job I wasn't sure I liked. I had rented a place to live that I couldn't really afford, and I was sleeping on a mattress on the floor because I didn't have the money to buy furniture. Then I discovered my new home was infested with fleas.

I took all my clothes to the laundromat a few blocks from where my new job was located and put them in a washing machine. I ran out of my office an hour later and put my clothes in the dryer, then ran back to the office. When I went out again an hour later to get my clothes out of the dryer, I discovered that someone had stolen them.

I still remember, many years later, what it felt like going back to work. I sat quietly in my office at the company I had joined less than a week ago. My head was in my hands. I had no friends or family for hundreds of miles. I felt very vulnerable and very alone. I had to figure out on my own why all these things were happening and what to do about them. Why did I seem to be making a series of bad decisions? Should I have taken the job? Should I have moved so far from friends and family? Why did I rent such an expensive place to live in when I couldn't afford it?

Then I had an *a-ha* moment.

In the 10 years before the current crisis, I had some tough times, including both of my parents dying. I had to be strong and independent and take care of myself. I had a belief that said, "I am a strong person. I can handle any crisis." I realized that I was (unconsciously) making decisions that would eventually cause more crises, at least partly so I could overcome them to prove to myself that I was strong. I had a belief that I was a strong person who could overcome all obstacles. I had a persona of a strong, independent person. That persona had been helpful and useful. I'd had a series of setbacks and I needed to think of myself as strong in order to make it through.

But the persona and the story around it had outlived its usefulness. The story and persona had become problems. I realized that I needed to change the story so I could change my persona. I knew that if I could change both my story and my persona, then I would start to make different decisions. And, in turn, those decisions would result in an easier life with fewer obstacles. I would find myself making decisions that resulted in easier and more pleasant outcomes.

I said out loud, "My life is easy and graceful." I took a few minutes and wrote down how my life was going to be different, about the type of person I would need to be in order for my life to be easy and graceful, about the things I would do differently if I were the kind of person who had an easy and graceful life. I would ask people for help—not just friends and family, but even people I didn't know well. I wrote a new story for my new persona.

One of my new coworkers walked by my office, leaned her head in and said, "How's it going?" The old persona would have put on a brave face and said, "Great, it's all great!" But the new persona said, "Well, actually, not so well."

I proceeded to tell her the story of the fleas and the laundromat. It turned out that she had an extra bedroom in her apartment, and she invited me to stay there while I got everything sorted out. I called my landlord. He tried fumigating the place while I stayed with my coworker. When he wasn't successful in getting rid of the fleas, I talked him into letting me out of the lease. My coworker became a friend, and suggested that I move in with her instead of looking for another place. I saved money and gained a new friend. She helped me adjust to my new city, and introduced me to her friends. I began to make decisions that would make my life easier. And, in fact, my life turned around and did get a lot easier. I learned how to ask for help and rely on others. I had changed my story. I had changed my persona. I was no longer a "strong person ready to handle crises." I was a "person ready to accept help and depend on friends."

Now there's research that proves the power of stories to shape personal stories, personas, and, by extension, to change beliefs, behaviors, and lives. In his book *Redirect: The Surprising New Science of Psychological Change* (Wilson 2011), Timothy Wilson talks about the research on "story editing." Here's the definition from his book:

> a set of techniques designed to redirect people's narratives about themselves and the social world in a way that leads to lasting changes in behavior.

I didn't realize it when I was going through my experience with the fleas and the laundromat, but I was using story editing to change my behavior. I had used story editing on myself.

What about with other people? Can you use story editing with other people to get them to do stuff? The answer is yes.

In this chapter we'll talk about how to use story editing, as well as another technique, story prompting, to get people to do stuff. You'll learn about how to use stories to influence people and why stories are so powerful. We'll also talk about personas—self-descriptions that are intertwined with the stories we tell about ourselves to ourselves and to others. You'll learn how to work with existing personas to get people to do stuff, and how to get people to change their personas.

It's hard to change behavior when you're working against someone's existing persona. In many of the chapters in this book you're working to get people to do stuff with methods that don't actually change the person's own view of who he or she is. But the strategies in this chapter will help you activate or even change an existing persona to get people to take certain actions. The easiest way by far to get people to do stuff is to get them to change their own story. Getting people to change their story, and thereby change their persona, is the most powerful and long-lasting way to get people to do stuff.

I Feel Your Pain (Literally!)

When we read or hear a story, our brains react partly as though we're experiencing the story ourselves.

A story contains a large amount of information in digestible chunks. Stories break down events into smaller units so we can better understand the information being communicated.

When you hear the word "storyteller," you might think of some overly dramatic person telling a story to children using different voices. But everyone is a storyteller.

Think about your communication with other people throughout a typical day. You wake up in the morning and tell your family about a dream you had (story). At work you tell a coworker about what happened at the new product design meeting the day before (story). At lunch you tell your friend about a family reunion you have coming up and your plans to take time off to go (story). After work you speak with your neighbor about the dog you encountered while you were on your evening walk (story).

Most of the communication in our daily lives is in the form of a story. Yet we rarely stop and think about stories and storytelling. Storytelling is so ubiquitous that we don't even realize we're doing it. If someone at work suggested you attend a workshop on how to communicate clearly at work, you might be interested. But you might scoff if someone suggested that you attend a workshop on storytelling. It's interesting how unaware and unappreciative most people are about the major way we communicate.

Stories involve many parts of the brain. When we're reading or listening to a story, there are many parts of our brain that are active:

- The auditory part of the new brain that deciphers sound (if the story is being listened to)
- Vision and text processing (if the story is being read)
- All the visual parts of the brain (as we imagine the characters in the story)
- And, often, the emotional part of the midbrain.

A story not only conveys information, it allows us to feel what the character in the story feels. Tania Singer's research on empathy (Singer 2004) studied the parts of the brain that react to pain.

First, she used fMRI scans to see what parts of the brain were active when participants experienced pain. She discovered that there were some parts of the brain that processed where the pain came from and how intense the pain really was. Other parts of the brain separately processed how unpleasant the pain felt and how much the pain bothered the person feeling it.

Then she asked participants to read stories about people experiencing pain. When participants read stories about someone in pain, the parts of the brain that processed where the pain comes from and how intense it is were not active, but the other areas that process how unpleasant the pain is *were* active.

We literally experience at least a part of other people's pain when we hear a story about pain. Likewise, we experience at least a part of other people's joy, sadness, confusion, and knowledge.

Stories are how we understand each other's experience.

Anecdotes versus Stories

Because of the way our brains react to stories, stories are the best way to communicate information. We're more likely to be committed, take action, and make a decision if we've experienced something concretely ourselves. Stories simulate actual experience. If you tell people a story, they're more likely to be willing to take action on the information than if you just present data.

Let's say you have to make a presentation to the department heads at work about your latest conversations with your customers. You want the group to agree to fund a new project based on the data. You interviewed 25 customers and surveyed another 100, and have lots of important data to share. Then you're going to ask for funding.

Your first thought might be to present a summary of the data in a numerical/statistical/data-driven format, for example:

- 75 percent of the customers we interviewed…
- Only 15 percent of the customers responding to the survey indicated…

But this data-based approach will be less persuasive than stories and anecdotes. You may want to include the data, but your presentation will be more powerful if you focus on one or more anecdotes, such as, "Mary M from San Francisco shared the following story about how she uses our product"; and then go on to tell Mary's story.

STRATEGIES

Strategy 29: People are more likely to do what you ask of them when you communicate your supporting information and data in the form of a story.

Our Internal Stories Drive Our Behavior

We think in stories. And the stories that we tell ourselves about ourselves influence our behavior.

Here's an example:

Someone knocks on your door. You recognize him as a kid from your neighborhood. He's selling popcorn as a fundraiser for a club he belongs to at school. The club is trying to go to the state convention. How do you react?

It depends on the story, or persona, you have of yourself when it comes to topics such as school, fundraising, and your relationship to your neighborhood. Here's one story you might relate to:

> I'm a very busy person. When I'm at home I want to relax, not get bombarded with people at the door selling things. I don't like it when people bother me at home with these fundraising schemes. The schools should pay for these trips and not make us buy this overpriced popcorn. This poor kid isn't to blame, but I'm not going to buy the popcorn because it just perpetuates this behavior. Someone has got to act right on this. I'm the kind of person who does what is right on principle. I'm going to say no nicely, but firmly.

Or maybe you can relate to this story:

> Oh, isn't that great that the kids are going to the state convention. I remember when I went on a similar trip when I was in high school. It was really fun. Maybe not all that educational, but definitely fun! I'm the kind of person who encourages students to have lots of experiences outside of our own neighborhood. I am the kind of person who supports the school. I'll buy some popcorn and help this kid out.

Or maybe you can relate to this story:

> It kind of annoys me that there are always these kids selling things. But this is part of being a good neighbor. I'm part of the community. I am a good citizen of our neighborhood. I'll buy the popcorn because that's what a good community member would do.

Multiple Personalities

We have an idea of who we are and what's important to us. Essentially we have a "story" operating about ourselves at all times. These self-stories, or personas, exert a powerful influence on our decisions and actions.

We actually have more than one persona. There are different personas for different aspects of life in relation to others. For example, we have a persona as a husband or wife, another persona as a parent, another persona at work, and yet another persona that defines our relationship with the neighborhood we live in.

The Desire to be Consistent

We make decisions based on staying true to our personas. Most of this decision making based on personas happens unconsciously. We strive to be consistent. We want to make decisions that match our idea of who we are. When we make a decision or act in a way that fits one of our personas, the decision or action will feel right. When we make a decision or act in a way that doesn't fit with one of our personas, we feel uncomfortable.

Once we make one decision consistent with one of the personas, we'll try to stay consistent with that persona. We'll be more likely to make a decision or take an action if it's consistent with that story or persona.

In the next sections we'll look at how to use this desire for consistency to get people to do stuff.

 STRATEGIES

Strategy 30: When you get people to change their own persona stories, they'll change their behaviors.

How to Turn on a Persona

Since personas are so powerful in governing decisions and behavior, you can influence whether someone does something and exactly what they do by activating an existing persona. You can activate a persona and connect the persona to specific action. This is a powerful way to get people to take action. Here's an example:

Jeffrey is in charge of local fundraising for one of his favorite charities, Lend a Hand for Jobs. Lend a Hand for Jobs helps people who are having a hard time getting a job. The organization provides job interview training, business clothes for interviewing, and helps people land a job. Jeffrey is going to give a presentation to a local business group, and hopes to get the group to agree to donate money to the charity.

Jeffrey prepares a presentation about all the wonderful things that the charity is doing, and examples of the people who have been helped. He's got great photos of the people they've helped and hopes that after showing the photos and telling the success stories, the local business group will vote to make a donation. Will he be successful? Will they donate money? How much?

Jeffrey is more likely to get the local business group to donate and more likely to get more money if he activates a persona. What personas do the decision makers in the local business group have that would make them want to donate and donate more? Here are some possibilities:

1. "I'm the type of person who gives a helping hand to others in need. In fact, that's why I'm a member of this local business group, because the group likes to help out people in our community who are in need."

2. "I am a successful business person. In fact, I'm so successful that I can afford to give back to the community. This local business group that I'm a member of is filled with other successful business people just like me. We are the cream of the crop."

3. "I struggled and worked hard to get to where I am. It wasn't easy. At one point I was unsuccessful and in trouble. Because other people were willing to help me, I was able to pull myself up to be successful. This local business group that I'm a member of is filled with other people like me who were once in difficult straits."

4. "I struggled and worked hard to get to where I am. It wasn't easy. At one point I was unsuccessful and in trouble. No one was willing to help me. I had to do it all by myself. But now that I've made it, I don't like to think

about those hard days. This local business group that I'm a member of is filled with successful business people who didn't struggle like I did. I want to forget about my previous life. I'm on top and that's all that matters."

Jeffrey's plan for the presentation and asking for a donation may not be successful with all of these personas. Let's take a look at how his plan will work for each persona and what he might want to do differently.

His plan will probably work fairly well with the first persona. But he can strengthen his presentation by first giving examples of other donations the local business group has made to similar charitable organizations. This would remind them of the first persona. By talking about similar donations, and then telling stories of the people in need, Jeffrey would be activating this "Gives a Helping Hand" persona. When he asks for money, he'll be more likely to get a yes, and more likely to get more money.

Jeffrey's plan will be less successful with the second persona, who is only partially activated by talking about people in need. Instead of highlighting all the wonderful things the local business group has done in the past to help people in need, Jeffrey should first talk about all the wonderful accomplishments the individual people in the group have had in their own successful businesses. He should include some stories about famous people in the world who have given back to others after achieving their own business success. Activating this "Cream of the Crop" persona is more likely to result in a donation, and a higher donation.

Jeffrey's plan is a good starting point for the third persona, but it's important that he also include specific stories about what happened to individuals in the program. He needs to have stories that show how a person who was once struggling makes it to success. Stories like this will activate this "Pulled Up by the Bootstraps" persona.

The toughest sell will be to the fourth persona. In fact, this is such a hard sell that Jeffrey is unlikely to have success with this persona. He'll have to use some of the techniques later in this chapter, like story editing, to actually change this persona to a different one before he can expect positive results.

The more that Jeffrey can tailor the message to activate one of the personas, the more successful he will be. Ideally Jeffrey would be making a one-on-one pitch to people he knows well. He could then customize the message to fit the persona of that individual.

He is, however, probably making a presentation to the whole group. The more people he knows in the group, the more he can anticipate likely personas and change his message, stories, and presentation to fit. The less he knows about the people in the group, the more he'll have to guess about likely personas. Jeffrey is unlikely to be able to build the presentation to activate four or more different personas, but he could certainly plan the presentation to fit at least two or even three, and he should do this if he wants to maximize the likelihood and size of donations for his charity.

Activating an existing persona and targeting a message to that persona is a powerful and relatively easy way to get people to do stuff. Changing someone's persona, however, is a little more complicated. Because people like to be consistent in their personas, it's trickier to get someone to change an existing persona. But it's doable. The next section will show you how to change an existing persona.

STRATEGIES

Strategy 31: Before you ask people to do something, activate a persona that's connected to what you want them to do.

The "Crack" Strategy

In the previous section you learned that people want to stay consistent with their personas, and that one of the easiest ways to get people to do stuff is to first activate a persona that will effortlessly lead to the action you want them to take.

But we also saw that sometimes people don't have a persona that fits with what you want them to do. If you try to fight a strong, existing persona you won't get very far in getting people to do stuff. But it is possible to change a persona.

I'm writing this book in 2013 on an Apple MacBook Pro laptop computer. That may not sound surprising, but it actually is. Here's the story:

I first started using computers in graduate school in the 1970s. I learned how to program large "mainframe" computers, as well as smaller "mini" computers (that weren't all that small!). When the personal computer revolution started up in the 1980s, I was right there. I even sold personal computers one year. Eventually I started my consulting career doing interface design and usability work for Fortune 1000 companies.

Fortune 1000 companies in the 1980s and 1990s used primarily Windows-based computers—and, as of this writing, they still do. Very few of my clients used Apple computers. "Serious" computer users were Windows based (or Unix based if you were really serious). Apple computers were for artists. If you were a "techie," you used a Windows-based PC. I was a techie. I was a PC person. My husband, however, was an Apple person. He was a newspaper editor, and he used Apple computers at work to lay out his newspaper pages.

Both my husband and I would archly defend our technology of choice. Over time, I learned to just ignore his comments about how horrible Windows PCs were, and how wonderful his Mac was. He learned to use a Windows-based PC, since our home computers were the cast-offs from my business. I was in charge of computers in our home, and they were all Windows-based machines. We learned to agree to disagree when it came to "what is the best computer." My persona was strongly rooted as a "savvy technology user."

Then Apple introduced the iPod. My children lobbied for us to buy them iPods and we did. Since I was a "savvy technology user," I bought an MP3 player, but I didn't buy an iPod. iPod was made by Apple. My persona didn't fit being an Apple fan. But my MP3 player was hard to use. The iPod was cool. My MP3 player was ugly and unusable.

So, I bought an iPod. I actually did feel a twinge of dissonance when I broke a little bit from my non-Apple, all-PC persona to buy an Apple product. But it was only a type of MP3 player really, right? So it was a small action outside my usual persona, nothing too drastic.

That was the crack.

I had introduced a crack in my PC persona. I was now a PC person who used an Apple product. I loved my iPod. And over time my PC persona began to give way. I was becoming a person who believed in Apple products. My persona began to shift, and a few years later, when my Windows-based laptop was past its prime and it came time to purchase a new computer, I bought a Mac laptop. Within a year or so I was all Apple.

Interestingly, I wasn't consciously aware of this whole process until my husband walked into my home office and stared. I was talking on my iPhone while typing on my Apple laptop. My iPad was next to me, and the Apple TV was on in the background. I had made an entire shift to Apple. When it comes to technology, I now have an Apple persona.

> ▶ **NOTE** Later in this chapter, in the "Start Small" section, we'll talk about why these small changes are so powerful.

I don't know if Apple planned to crack people's Windows PC personas by introducing a non-computer product, the iPod. But that has certainly been the effect for me, and likely many others.

Once a persona is established and active, it's easy to get people to take actions and make decisions that are consistent with that persona. If, however, the active persona is not consistent with what you want someone to do, you may need to figure out how to change the persona. If you launch an all-out assault on a person's persona to try and get them to radically change who they are from the outside (you are the outside), you will not succeed. But if you can introduce a small crack in the existing persona, you have an opportunity to have a new persona enter and take over.

In the sections on commitment, story editing, and story prompting that follow, you'll learn more about how to encourage personas to change.

 STRATEGIES

Strategy 32: When you introduce a small crack in an existing persona, you'll change the persona over time. When you change the persona, you can then change the behavior.

The "Anchor to a Persona" Strategy

What if you want to get people to do stuff, but there isn't an existing persona you can crack? Can you create a new persona?

If someone has an existing persona, you can use that as an anchor and more easily create a new persona from it.

What if someone knocked on your door and asked if you would be willing to put a huge, and not very well constructed, billboard in your front yard that said in large block lettering DRIVE CAREFULLY.

Do you think you would agree? Well, most people in Palo Alto, California who were asked to do so in a research study in 1966 said no.

Jonathan Freedman and Scott Fraser (Freedman 1966) had a researcher pose as a volunteer and go door to door asking homeowners to allow just such a sign to be installed in their front yards. They were shown a photo of the sign that would be installed. The signs were quite large (they essentially would take over the front yard) and were fairly ugly. This was not an attractive object to have in their yards! Fewer than 20 percent agreed to have the signs installed in their yards. No surprise there. (Well, actually it is surprising that as many as 20 percent would agree at all.) That was the control group (Group A) of the experiment.

Here's how the rest of the experiment went:

Group B was created, comprising random people who were contacted by an experimenter who asked them to put a small (three-inch) sign in the back windows of their cars that said "Drive Carefully." Then, three weeks later, a different experimenter showed up to inquire about their interest in having a large DRIVE CAREFULLY sign installed in their yards.

Group C comprised people who were contacted by an experimenter who asked them to sign a petition to "Keep California Beautiful." Then, three weeks later, a different experimenter showed up to inquire about their interest in having a large DRIVE CAREFULLY sign installed in their yards.

In the control group (Group A) only 20 percent agreed to have the large DRIVE CAREFULLY signs installed in their yards. What about Groups B and C?

In Group B, which had been asked to first put the small Drive Carefully signs in their car windows and then were approached later to put the large signs in their yards, 76 percent said yes to the signs in their yards.

For Group C, which had been asked first to sign a petition to Keep California Beautiful (a totally different cause than Drive Carefully), 46 percent agreed to the big, ugly signs.

It's important to note that in both B and C, different experimenters returned to make the second request—people in those groups were not agreeing simply because they had a relationship of any sort with the person asking.

Twenty percent versus 46 percent. Twenty percent versus 76 percent. Why were people much more willing to put a big, ugly sign in their yards in these two other conditions?

The first reason has to do with activating an existing persona, as we discussed earlier in the chapter. By agreeing to the request to put the small Drive Carefully sign in the back windows of their cars, a persona was activated in Group B. They were telling themselves the story that they are a person who cares about the community at large; they are someone who cares about safety. So when they were later asked about installing the big, ugly signs, well, for most people that request now fit the persona they had about themselves.

But what about Group C? Group C people were first asked to sign a petition to "Keep California Beautiful," and later asked to put up the DRIVE CAREFULLY sign. The agreement was double that of Group A (46 percent, compared to 20 percent), but still not as high as the condition of Group B (76 percent).

That's because the petition activated a persona that says, "I'm a person who cares about the community," but didn't necessarily activate a persona that says, "I'm a person who cares about safety." The "I'm a person who cares about safety" is a new persona that was created from the original anchor persona. Because it's new, it's not as strong—but it's a start.

When you activate an existing persona, you then create an opening where a new but somewhat related persona can be introduced. When they were asked later to do something a little bit different (to install the huge DRIVE CAREFULLY sign in their yards), that request activated a new persona that was somewhat related to the existing persona. The original persona of "I'm a person who cares about the community" is different from "I'm a person who cares about safety." But the two are consistent, and easily connected.

You can use someone's existing persona as an anchor and more easily create a new persona from it. Make a request that activates the existing persona. After the person has agreed to that, then make a request that fits with the persona you are trying to create. Here are some examples of persona pairs:

- Existing persona: "I'm someone who takes care of my body."
- New persona that would be easy to create: "I'm someone who cares about healthy children."

- Existing persona: "I'm someone who is frugal with money."
- New persona that would be easy to create: "I'm someone who votes to keep down government debt."

- Existing persona: "I'm someone who is creative."
- New persona that would be easy to create: "I'm someone who likes to try new things."

In the next section we'll expand on this idea by showing how to get small commitments, even to actions that are inconsistent with existing personas.

 STRATEGIES

Strategy 33: To get people to do something, use an existing persona and anchor a new—but related—persona to it.

Start Small

Small actions, over time, can lead to large persona change. In the previous section we showed how you can create new personas by anchoring them to existing personas. In that case we were using an existing persona as an anchor.

But what if you want people to make a decision or take an action and there isn't an existing related persona you can anchor to? Can you get someone to do something that is inconsistent with an existing persona?

The answer is yes, but you have to start small. Remember my story earlier in this chapter about switching from a Windows PC persona to an Apple persona? I had a persona that I was a Windows person. If someone had started by suggesting that I become an Apple person, I would have laughed. If someone suggested I buy an Apple laptop, I would have said no. All these requests were too large. My persona was "I am a Windows person." It's unlikely that I would make a big switch from "I am a Windows person" to "I am an Apple person" in one leap. If we want people to make big changes like this, we have to start with small actions.

What does small mean? Small is an action that, even though it's inconsistent with an existing persona, doesn't set off alarm bells. A small action request doesn't make me feel that I'm going against an existing persona.

If the action is small, it's possible for people to take an action that is inconsistent with a strong, existing persona. Once they take *that* action, they actually will adjust their persona a little to fit the new action they just took.

When we take a small action that's inconsistent with an existing persona, it actually starts a new persona. We probably aren't aware that this has happened. But now that the new persona exists, the next thing we're asked to do along those same lines will fit the new persona, and it will be easier for us to continue to take action consistent with this new, revised persona.

If you ask people to take small actions, then you can use this small commitment/stair-step approach to create a brand new persona. If you want someone to take action, you need to first get a commitment to something small. It can be something that fits with one of their existing personas, or something that's inconsistent with an existing persona. The more inconsistent it is, the smaller the action and commitment need to be.

For example, if Corinne thinks of herself as "someone who gives to charity," you might be able to get her to donate money and an hour or two of her time for the charity you're promoting. But if she thinks of herself as "someone who has pulled myself up like everyone should do," then you'll need to start really small. Instead of asking for both money and volunteer action, you'll have to start with just one of those.

Whether you're asking people to do something that fits with an existing persona or not, if you get people to take an action, even a small one, that action can lead to larger actions later on.

 STRATEGIES

Strategy 34: To change a persona, get people to take one small action that is inconsistent with their current persona.

Going Public

In the experiment described above from Freedman and Fraser, some of the participants put a sign in their car window. Their commitment (to driving carefully) was a public commitment. The more public a commitment people make, the stronger the influence that action has on future actions. The more public a commitment that people make, the stronger the persona change will be.

When we take an action that only we know about, we aren't showing our commitment. When we're not showing our commitment, there will be less long-term persona change than when we take an action that others see.

When the people in the Freedman experiment posted a sign in their yard or put a sticker in their car window, they were making a public commitment. Public commitments lead to stronger and faster persona change.

How to Get Public Commitment

Besides asking people to put signs up in their front yards, how can you get people to make a public commitment, and by doing so, make it more likely that they'll take even more action?

If someone has made any commitment at all to your organization, company, product, or service, you can strengthen that commitment by asking them to make a more public show of support.

As an example, let's say that you run a hotel chain. When customers stay at your hotel you send them a survey to fill out. This survey is a form of public commitment. If they rate your hotel well, then they have made a public commitment. Be sure to ask as one of the questions how likely they will be to stay at your hotel again. A survey can be a way for you to get data and feedback about your products and services, but it's also a way to get people to publicly commit.

You can even send a survey to people who are not yet customers or associated with your organization. If you ask them about their perceptions of your organization, products, or services, and they indicate positive responses, then they have just committed publicly and will be more open to dealing with you in the future.

The more public the commitment, the more it will stick—and the more it will affect your audience's current and future behavior. Asking your audience to complete an anonymous survey is better than getting no commitment at all, but asking them for a testimonial or recommendation, or asking them to write a review that is posted online, earns an even stronger show of commitment from your audience.

When people give a recommendation, testimonial, or write a review, they are saying, "I am a person who believes in this product," or "I am a person who donates to this organization," or "I am a person who buys from this company."

Reviews act on others as a form of social validation (see Chapter 2, "The Need To Belong"), but they also act on the self as a form of commitment. If we write a positive review, we'll then want to stay consistent, and that means we'll take more action to interact with the site, the company, the organization. If you want to build commitment to your brand, your company, or a product, then make sure you give visitors the opportunity to write a review.

Don't Pay People to Commit

Robert Cialdini (Cialdini 2006) reports that if a public commitment is not "owned" by a person but is instead made in order to gain a large reward, the individual is not deeply committed and will not show deep commitment in future behavior. If we believe that we have voluntarily chosen to act in a certain way because of our inner beliefs rather than strong outside pressures, we feel more committed. A large reward, for example, may lead us to act, but it will not create inner responsibility for the action and we won't feel committed.

 STRATEGIES

Strategy 35: When you get people to commit publicly, it's easier to get them to do stuff.

Strategy 36: Don't pay people for their commitments.

Writing Increases Commitment

When we write something down, especially longhand, then we're more committed to it. Writing compared to, for example, thinking or talking about something increases our commitment to the idea and to taking action.

Morton Deutsch and Harold Gerard (Deutsch 1955) asked people to estimate the length of some lines drawn on a piece of paper. They were looking at the effect that others' opinions might have on decision making. They had other people, who were part of the experiment, purposely estimate the length of the lines incorrectly.

Would the participants in the experiment go along with the incorrect estimates they were hearing from others, or would they stick (commit) to the answer they felt was correct?

What they found was that people would change their estimate of the line lengths based on what the other people in the room estimated. This goes along with the idea of social validation that we talk about in Chapter 2, "The Need To Belong."

But Deutsch and Gerard also looked at whether there were situations in which commitment to a decision would be stronger than in other situations. Before hearing what others had to say on the length of the line:

- Group 1 wrote their estimates on paper. They were told *not* to sign the paper, and that they would not be turning in the sheets of paper.
- Group 2 wrote their estimates on a "magic pad," and then lifted a sheet and the estimate was erased without anyone seeing it.
- Group 3 was told to write their estimates on paper and to sign the paper. They were told that their papers would be collected at the end of the experiment.

Did the groups vary in terms of how strongly they stuck to their commitment of the length of the line?

Group 2 was most likely to change their decisions and to give incorrect estimates. Groups 1 and 3 were both five times less likely to change their answers. They were more committed to their original estimates, regardless of what they heard others say.

Signing their names or being told they were going to hand in their estimates did *not* seem to make a difference. Just the act of writing it on something relatively permanent was enough to make them commit.

Writing Longhand Changes the Brain

When I wrote my Ph.D. thesis in graduate school, my first draft was done by hand (OK, now I've admitted that I'm quite old!). Most writing these days is done by typing on a keyboard. I'm writing this book on my laptop, and most of my communication with friends and family is done via emails that I, of course, compose at my laptop keyboard. There are still a few things I write by hand—my most important daily to-do lists are done by hand, as well as most of my business planning. It's interesting, when you stop to think about it, which things you write by hand versus on a keyboard. But does it matter?

Research by Reza Shadmehr and Henry Holcomb (Shadmehr 1997) looked at brain activity when people wrote longhand (for example, with a pen or pencil) as opposed to typing on a keyboard. Writing involves different muscles than typing, and Shadmehr and Holcomb found that there was more memory consolidation when people were writing in longhand.

 STRATEGIES

Strategy 37: When people write their commitments longhand, they are more committed.

Prompt a New Story

In the beginning of this chapter I related my experience with how I changed my story of being a "strong survivor" to someone who has an "easy and graceful" life. In his book *Redirect*, Timothy Wilson describes a large body of impressive research on how stories can change behavior in the long term. Wilson calls this technique "story editing."

If you can get people to rewrite their story related to what it is you want them to do, this is likely to result in large and long-term change. Story editing has been used to help with post-traumatic stress disorder, and with teens at risk. But it can also be effective in getting an employee to come in to work on time, or to switch from being a solo "hot dog" to being a collaborative team player.

The technique of story editing is so simple that it doesn't seem possible that it can result in such deep and profound change. In other chapters I describe some strategies for getting people to do stuff that are a lot of work, even to change a somewhat simple behavior. If it's that much work to change a simple behavior, then how can it be easy to change a whole life in a few minutes?

Story editing is so powerful that it can seem like magic, but it's not. When we write a new story that describes who we are, why we behave as we do, and how we relate to others, that story changes our persona, and we will, consciously and unconsciously, start to make decisions and act in ways that are consistent with that story. You also now know that it's even more powerful if you can get someone to write out the story on paper, in longhand.

But what if you can't get someone to stop, think, and write out a new story? Does that mean that you can't use the powerful effect of stories? Luckily the answer is you still can use stories to change behavior. Even if you can't get someone to sit down and write out a new story, you can provide a story for them, and that's almost as good.

Here's an example from Wilson's research on college students:

Some college students were not doing well in their first year of school. The students were getting low grades on one or more tests, and had started thinking things like "I'm in over my head," "Maybe I don't belong at this college," or "I'm not smart enough."

The students were falling into a self-defeating story about themselves. Because they began to believe that they were in over their heads, they started behaving that way. They stopped studying and started skipping classes. This, of course, resulted in more low grades, and convinced them further that they couldn't be successful.

Not all students react this way when they have trouble. Some students might create a different story, for example: "This course is harder than I thought it would be," "I guess my high school work didn't prepare me well enough for this class," or "I'm going to have to work harder, study more, maybe get a tutor." These students' stories led to more studying and getting more help, and therefore better grades.

But here's the question. Without asking students to write out a new story for themselves, can you quickly prompt a story for the "self-defeating" students that is more empowering and hopeful?

Wilson had the students with the self-defeating stories come in to participate in an experiment. They thought they were being asked to take a survey of first year students' attitudes about college life. Wilson told them that they would see the results from earlier surveys of older students, so they would know what kind of questions would be on their survey. In actuality

Wilson was showing them the previous survey results in order to prompt them with a new story.

The student participants then saw survey results of these older students that showed that many of the students had problems with grades during their first year, but that their grades improved over time. They watched video interviews of four older students who told the story about how they realized that the course work was harder than they thought it would be, and that they had to work harder, study more, and get help.

The students in the videos talked about their grades steadily increasing over time.

Altogether the participants spent 30 minutes hearing from other students who had problems with low grades, but then improved their grades. That was all they did. They didn't get any counseling or learn about better study habits. They just heard a different story.

The participants didn't know that the purpose of the study was to improve their grades. What Wilson hoped was that he had prompted a new story, even if the participants were not aware of it. He hoped that he had prompted a story such as "Maybe it's not hopeless. Maybe I'm like those other students. They tried harder and were able to raise their grades. Maybe I can, too."

The story prompting worked. Wilson reports that the participants achieved better grades in the following year than a randomly assigned control group who did not get the story prompting. The participants were also less likely to drop out of college.

Thirty minutes of reading and watching videos resulted in students working harder, improving their grades, and staying in school.

You can get people to change their behavior in big ways, and with a small amount of effort, if you can do a reasonably good job at

- Guessing the current story that is currently operating and currently influencing their behavior
- Coming up with an alternate story
- Figuring out a way to expose them to the new story

With story prompting, Wilson doesn't talk about the difference between telling people a new story versus letting them "discover" the story on their own. But my sense is that the latter is better. The key is that people have to change their own story. If you just give them another story and say, "Here's the story you have and here's the story you should have," it likely has less impact than letting them discover a new story for themselves and comparing it to a story they may not even realize they have. With story prompting, it's more effective to tell them a story about someone else and let them draw the parallels. Sometimes less is more!

 STRATEGIES

Strategy 38: Expose people to the stories of others so they'll be encouraged to create new stories for themselves.

5

Carrots and Sticks

WE'RE GOING TO START with dog saliva.

Ivan Pavlov was born in 1849 in a village in Russia. His father was a priest, and Ivan also started seminary school, but left to go to university and study natural science. He started researching digestion using animals. He was a prolific and serious scientist. In all the pictures of Pavlov he has a huge bushy beard and a stern expression. In 1904 he won the Nobel Prize in medicine.

While Pavlov was doing his research on digestion he discovered something that surprised him. He was measuring the amount of saliva that dogs produce as part of digestion. He noticed that the dogs would start salivating before they started eating. They would actually salivate as soon as they saw the food.

Then he noticed that, before the food even arrived, the dogs would start salivating when they heard a bell over the door to the building ring as the researchers were bringing in the food. They would start salivating when they heard the footsteps of the person who was coming to feed them. The food was being paired with something else, like footsteps, or bells. Pavlov started a series of experiments around these automatic reactions to stimuli. He called the automatic reaction "classical conditioning." Here's how it works:

First, you pair two things together—a stimulus (food) and a response (salivating):

Stimulus (Food) → Response (Salivating)

Then you add an additional stimulus:

Stimulus 1 (Food) + Stimulus 2 (Bell) → Response (Salivating)

Over time you'll be able to remove the original stimulus, and have just the additional stimulus elicit the response:

Stimulus 2 (Bell) → Response (Salivating)

But what does any of this have to do with getting people to do stuff? After all, you're probably not trying to get someone to salivate!

Getting People to Do Stuff Automatically

Classical conditioning is the starting point for understanding automatic behavior. One way to get people to do stuff is to get the "stuff" to be automatic.

It's much easier for people to do things if they just automatically do them. A lot of behavior is actually the same as Pavlov's classical conditioning.

I use classical conditioning when I teach classes. I teach one- and two-day classes at Fortune 1000 companies and nonprofits, and I teach college classes. When I teach I like to build in lots of short breaks.

During the breaks people are outside in the hall talking, or in the room checking email and texting. But when the break is over I want people to come back in the room and be ready to learn again. I use classical conditioning. When it's break time I play music and open the door to the room.

When the break is over I turn off the music and move toward the door to close it:

> *Stimulus 1 (Instructor says "OK, Let's pick up where we left off") → Response (People take seats and get quiet)*

Then we add

> *Stimulus 1 (Instructor says "OK, Let's pick up where we left off") → Stimulus 2 (Music is turned off and/or instructor moves toward the door to close it) → Response (People take seats and get quiet)*

Until we get

> *Stimulus 2 (Music is turned off and/or instructor moves toward the door to close it) → Response (People take seats and get quiet)*

Here's another one: I want people to participate in discussions and speak up when I walk to the flip chart or whiteboard and ask a question:

> *Stimulus 1 (Instructor says, "What do you think? Does anyone have an idea?") → Response (People speak up with ideas)*

Then we add

> *Stimulus 1 (Instructor says, "What do you think? Does anyone have an idea?" → Stimulus 2 (Instructor walks to the flip chart or whiteboard, takes cap off a marker, and looks at class with raised eyebrows) → Response (People speak up with ideas)*

Until we get

Stimulus 2 (Instructor walks to the flip chart or whiteboard, takes cap off a marker, and looks at class with raised eyebrows) → Response (People speak up with ideas)

Now you know two of my classroom management secrets!

STRATEGIES

Strategy 39: Once people become conditioned to do something, you can pair a new stimulus to the behavior you want and get people to respond automatically.

What the Casinos Know

What do these people have in common?

- A high school student who gets money for every A she brings home
- An employee who gets a raise every year
- A customer who gets a free cup of coffee for every 10 cups of coffee he buys
- A vacationer who puts token after token into a slot machine in Las Vegas

Their behavior is being shaped according to the principles of B. F. Skinner.

When I see people sitting in a casino putting money into slot machines and pushing buttons, all I can think about is Skinner's experiments. I know some of you reading this might like casinos, gambling, and Las Vegas and will say, "There's more to Las Vegas than slot machines." So I'll try not to offend you in this section of the book.

But I do want to talk about the powerful theories of behavior analysis from the 1950s and why you have to understand how behavior analysis works if you're going to get people to do stuff.

In the 1950s, Skinner added a new dimension to Pavlov's classical conditioning ideas. Rather than focusing just on the stimulus and response, Skinner started experimenting with rats and pigeons on how rewards influence behavior. He called it "operant" conditioning (as opposed to Pavlov's "classical" conditioning).

Skinner didn't use the word "reward" very much. He preferred to call a reward a "reinforcement." There's a reason for that, which we'll get to shortly.

Here was Skinner's idea: If you want to increase a specific behavior, then you reinforce (reward) that behavior. If you want to decrease a specific behavior, then you don't reinforce that behavior. It sounds like common sense, but Skinner took it beyond common sense to find the science underneath it. Here is Skinner's basic idea:

Behavior → Reinforcement → More of that behavior

For example:

Get an A on your report card at school → Get $5 → Get more A's

Or

Push a button → Win money from the machine → Push the button more

Or

Turn the report in on time → Get praise: "Great job meeting that deadline!" → Submit more reports on time

Skinner went further and researched questions such as what kind of reinforcement you should give, when you should give it, how often, and how much. If you want people to do stuff, you need to know some of these subtle but critical details of human behavior.

Think about it: You're trying to get someone to do something, like take out the garbage, write a report, or go vote. And you're racking your brain trying to figure out how to do that. "Maybe I should give him (or her) an incentive," you think. "Should it be cash or something else?"

In the meantime there are thousands of people sitting in casinos, right at this moment, and they're not being paid to do stuff (press a button). In fact, they're paying someone else for the privilege of pressing the button (and most of the time losing their money). Looking at it this way, are you curious about what the casinos know that maybe you should know?

We'll come back to casinos, but first let's talk about rats.

Choose from Five Basic Schedules of Reinforcement

Let's say you put a rat in a cage with a bar. If the rat presses the bar, he gets a food pellet. The food pellet is the reinforcement:

Behavior → Reinforcement → More of that behavior

In this case it looks like this:

Push a button → Get a food pellet → Push the button more

But what if you set it up so that the rat does not get the food pellet every time he presses the bar?

Skinner endlessly tested out various scenarios, and found that he could predict and control how often and how fast the rats pressed the bar to get the food pellet. There were differences in the amount and rate of the bar pressing based on how often he gave the food pellet, and whether he gave it based on elapsed time or the number of bar presses.

He called these differences "schedules." There are five basic schedules:

- **Continuous reinforcement.** You provide a food pellet every time the rat presses the bar.
- **Fixed interval.** You provide a food pellet after a certain interval of time has passed, for example, five minutes. The rat gets a food pellet the first time he presses the bar after five minutes is up.
- **Variable interval.** You provide a food pellet after an interval of time has passed, but the time interval varies. Sometimes it's one minute, sometimes five, sometimes three, and so on.
- **Fixed ratio.** Instead of basing the reinforcement on time, you base it on the number of bar presses. The rat gets a food pellet after every 10 bar presses, or after every 5 presses. Reinforcement is based on the number of bar presses, and the number is always the same.
- **Variable ratio.** Reinforcement is based on the number of bar presses, but the number of presses required to get the food pellet varies. Sometimes the food pellet comes after 5 presses, sometimes 10, sometimes 3, and so on.

It turns out that rats (and people) behave in predictable ways based on the schedule being used. You'll learn how to use these schedules to affect behavior in the following sections.

STRATEGIES

Strategy 40: It's not enough to just give a reward. You need to decide which type of schedule to use if you want the reward to be effective in getting people to do stuff.

Continuous Reinforcement: How to Get People to Do Something New

If you give your daughter money every time she receives a grade of A at the end of a semester class, then you're using a continuous reinforcement schedule. Every time she gets the A (produces the desired behavior) she gets money (money is the reinforcement).

If you praise your employees every time they hand in a report on time, then you're using a continuous reinforcement schedule. Every time the report is produced on time (desired behavior), you give praise (praise is the reinforcement).

Continuous reinforcement is best when you're trying to establish a new behavior, but once established, you should switch to one of the other schedules.

When you use continuous reinforcement, you will initially see a lot of the behavior as the person (or rat, or dog) learns the behavior. But over time the desired behavior will become intermittent. And the down side is that if you remove the reinforcement (that is, stop paying the money for every A, or don't praise the behavior every time) the desired behavior is likely to stop too.

STRATEGIES

Strategy 41: When you're trying to establish a new behavior, give a reward every time the person does the behavior (continuous reinforcement).

Strategy 42: Once a behavior is established with continuous reinforcement, switch to a different reward schedule to keep the behavior going.

Variable Ratio: How to Get People to Keep Doing It

When an employee receives praise sometimes, but not others, that's a variable ratio schedule.

When a player wins at the slot machine after playing 56 rounds, that's a variable ratio schedule. Most casino games are based on a variable ratio schedule. The player pulls the slot machine lever 10 times and gets a reward, then plays 52 more rounds before the next reward.

From the employee's or player's point of view, variable ratio schedules are unpredictable. The reinforcement is based on how many times the person does the behavior, but it changes all the time. The person doesn't know if she'll get the reward the next time she does the behavior, or after 30 times, 5 times, or 100 times.

Because the person doesn't know when the next reinforcement will come, she'll do the behavior over and over.

This means that variable ratio schedules tend to stick. If you remove the reinforcement, the behavior will continue for a long time. Psychologists would say that the behavior is "resistant to extinction" on a variable ratio schedule.

 STRATEGIES

Strategy 43: When you want a behavior to stick, give rewards on a variable ratio schedule.

Variable Interval: How to Get Stable Behavior

George runs a lab that's subject to periodic government inspections. He knows the inspector is going to stop by, but he doesn't know when. It might be this month, in three months, or in six months. The inspector likes to do surprise inspections.

So George decides he'd better make sure the lab meets all the requirements all the time so he can get an "excellent" rating when the inspector does stop by. In this case, following all the regulations and requirements is the desired behavior, and getting an "excellent" rating is the reinforcement.

The inspector comes periodically (based on time), but not on a predictable, fixed interval. So this is a variable interval schedule. We can expect that George will do a fairly good job of meeting the inspection requirements most of the time because he's on a variable interval schedule, and that he'll continue to show the desired behavior over a long period of time (that is, behaviors are resistant to extinction on a variable interval schedule).

When your goal is to have people do something regularly, but not necessarily a lot, then a variable interval schedule is a good one to use.

George will likely review his lab procedures and do his own inspection once a month to make sure everything is ready in case the lab inspector comes by, but he won't engage in this behavior every day. Doing a lot of internal reviews doesn't, in the long run, result in more reward (as a variable ratio schedule would). So we're unlikely to see a lot of the behavior, but we *will* see it steadily and see it regularly.

The variable interval schedule is not a good one to use to establish a new behavior, however, because rewards don't come frequently enough to establish the relationship between the behavior and the reward. You'll need to use continuous reinforcement at first and then switch to the variable interval schedule once the behavior is established.

STRATEGIES

Strategy 44: Use a variable interval schedule when you don't need a lot of a certain behavior; you simply want to see the behavior steadily and regularly.

Fixed Ratio: How to Get a Burst of Behavior

Let's say you own a coffee shop and you have a frequent buyer card for your customers. For every 10 coffees a customer buys, she gets one free. She gets her card stamped every time she gets a coffee. This is a fixed ratio schedule.

Research tells us that this will result in a burst of behavior (the customer will buy a lot of coffee over a short period of time to fill up the card), but then, after getting her free coffee, there will be a lull and there will be less behavior (she will buy less coffee from that coffee shop).

People Are More Motivated as They Get Closer to a Goal

There isn't much you can do to prevent the lull after people reach the goal. You can have them start all over (give them another, blank card to fill up with coffee stamps), or you can have another level for them to reach with even better rewards. There is something you can do, however, to speed up their behavior.

Ran Kivetz (Kivetz 2006) did an experiment with frequent buyer coffee cards. He gave some people Card A and some people Card B:

- **Card A** had 10 boxes for the stamps; when the participants got the card, all the boxes were blank.
- **Card B** had 12 boxes for the stamps; when the participants got the card, the first two boxes were already stamped.

How long did it take to get the card filled up? Did it take longer or shorter for Card A versus Card B? The participants had to buy 10 cups of coffee with either card in order to get the free coffee. So did one card result in different behavior than the other?

The answer apparently was yes. People with Card B filled up the card faster than those with Card A, even though both cards required ten coffees to reach the end.

The reason is called the *goal-gradient effect*. The goal-gradient effect was first studied with rats in 1934 by Clark Hull (Hull 1934). He found that rats that were running a maze to get food at the end would run faster as they got to the end of the maze.

The goal-gradient effect says that people will accelerate their behavior as they progress closer toward a goal. So when customers saw on Card B that they already had some progress toward the goal, even if they didn't drink those two coffees, they worked faster to fill up the rest of the card.

Kivetz also found that people enjoyed being part of a reward program. When compared to customers who were not part of the program, Kivetz found that the customers with reward cards smiled more, chatted longer with café employees, said "thank you" more often, and left a tip more often.

People Focus on What's Left More Than What's Completed

Here's a subtle but important note about using fixed ratio schedules. Minjung Koo (Koo 2010) conducted research to see which would motivate people more to reach a goal:

a. Focusing on what they'd already completed
b. Focusing on what remained to accomplish

The answer was b—people were more motivated to continue when they focused on what was left to do.

This means that if you use a fixed ratio schedule, then it's important to show people every step of the way how much they have left to reach the goal.

 STRATEGIES

Strategy 45: When you use a fixed ratio schedule, you'll get a burst of behavior, but it will drop off after the reward.

Strategy 46: When you use a fixed ratio schedule, people will be most motivated when you show them how much is left to reach the goal—not just how far they've come.

Why a Fixed Interval Schedule Isn't as Effective

When you give an employee a raise once a year, you have her on a fixed interval schedule. The tendency with a fixed interval schedule is for the person to not do much until she gets close to the moment when the reinforcement is coming. For example, you meet with your employee for an annual performance review, and at that time you agree on some performance improvements.

What will most likely happen is that the employee will make a few changes initially, but then fall back into old habits. When 11 months have gone by the employee will start to work on the performance improvements, because the next annual review and raise is about to happen. You have set up a fixed interval schedule, which is not a great schedule for getting consistent behavior.

Instead, start people with continuous reinforcement of the behaviors you want, and then move to one of the other schedules, for example, variable ratio or variable interval to work on performance changes.

 STRATEGIES

Strategy 47: Avoid giving rewards based on a fixed time interval. This schedule of reinforcement is less effective than other schedules.

SLOT MACHINES: PAVLOV AND SKINNER

Let's go back to those slot machines, which actually combine both Pavlov classical conditioning with Skinner operant conditioning:

Stimulus (bright lights and noises) → Behavior (Put in money and press button) → Sometimes get reinforcement A (money)

Stimulus (bright lights and noises) → Behavior (Put in money and press button) → Always get reinforcement B (bright lights and noises)

The casinos are using the reinforcement for one (bright lights and noises) as the stimulus for another. This causes an addictive loop:

Stimulus (bright lights and noises) → Behavior (Put in money and press button) → Always get reinforcement B (bright lights and noises, which now become the next stimulus) → Behavior (Put in money and press button) → Sometimes get reinforcement A (money) and always get reinforcement B (bright lights and noises), and so on.

Casino owners are smart. It works.

Rewarding Baby Steps

There's a story that makes the rounds in psychology classes about how a class of students at a college used the operant idea of "shaping" to get the professor to leave the classroom in the middle of his lecture. The students arranged this among themselves ahead of time, before class started.

They planned to give a succession of reinforcements. First, when the professor came in to start the class, the students ignored him (no reinforcement), until he looked toward the door. At some point in the lecture he randomly looked toward the door. When he did, the students looked at him attentively for a moment.

Every time he looked toward the door they would look up attentively. Looking up attentively was the reinforcement. Professors love it when students seem interested and attentive in class.

Before too long the professor was looking at the door a lot. On a secret signal from one student in the class, the whole group would then stop reinforcing looking toward the door. Instead, they would look up attentively only if the professor took a step toward the door. At some point in the lecture he took a step toward the door, and then the students looked up attentively.

This "shaping" of the professor's behavior continued (he moves closer to the door, he moves his arm toward the door, he touches the door, he turns the door handle, and so on) until the professor actually left the room.

I'm pretty sure it's an urban legend, created by a psychology professor who was trying to explain shaping, but it could happen!

The official description of shaping is "the differential reinforcement of successive approximations." We know with the principle of operant conditioning that any behavior we reinforce will increase. But if you're trying to establish a new behavior, you can't reinforce it yet, so you have to first reinforce an earlier behavior that will lead to the behavior you're looking for.

Once that earlier behavior is established using reinforcement, then you can stop reinforcing that behavior and reinforce only behavior that moves you closer to the final desired behavior.

Example: Shaping a "Wash Hands" Behavior

Katie manages a team of nurses at a hospital. She'd like to get one of the nurses, Joanne, to wash her hands more often. Hand washing is critical in patient care, but not all hospital staff are vigilant in doing it.

Katie has tried talking to Joanne about this, but so far Joanne's behavior hasn't changed. In fact, Katie thinks the more she mentions it, the less Joanne is washing. Katie decides to try shaping with Joanne.

She figures out a plan for shaping Joanne's behavior:

1. Katie starts by looking for situations to be around Joanne when there are hand-washing opportunities.

    Katie waits until she sees Joanne move toward the sink. As soon as she takes a step toward the sink, Katie smiles and starts talking to Joanne. At first she's just moving toward the sink randomly, but that doesn't matter.

If she's moving toward the sink at all, Katie smiles, and gives Joanne a compliment on something, for example, how well she handled the last patient. Katie knows that praise and conversation are two things that Joanne likes, and that these will be effective reinforcements for Joanne. Katie does this for a few days until the moving toward the sink behavior is established.

2. Katie looks for the next behavior in the shaping succession, which she has decided is not just moving toward the sink, but actually touching it.

    On the first day of the new shaping requirement, Katie doesn't say anything when Joanne moves toward the sink. But at one point Joanne touches the sink, and then Katie smiles and praises Joanne. Katie responds to the touching of the sink for several more days.

3. The last part of the shaping succession is to get Joanne to actually wash her hands. So Katie stops giving praise and conversation for touching the sink.

    She's quiet and waits for the time when Joanne actually turns on the water and lathers her hands. As soon as there is soap on Joanne's hands, Katie smiles and starts a conversation that includes praise. She'll continue to do this for a few more days to be sure the behavior is established.

At this point you might be saying, "Whew! What a lot of work to get to one small action." Shaping *is* a lot of work! And there are some critical components you have to get right if it's going to work:

- **Pay attention.** You have to be vigilant in looking for the behavior you want so you can identify every instance when the person does the desired behavior.

- **Give the right reinforcement every time (at first).** You have to give the reinforcement each time at the beginning. For Joanne the reinforcement was a combination of praise and conversation. As with any operant conditioning (shaping is a form of operant conditioning), you have to choose the reinforcement carefully. If you pick something that the person doesn't consider a reinforcement, then it won't work. For example, if you choose conversation with you as the reinforcement and the person doesn't like you, then conversation with you won't reinforce the behavior!

- **Give the reinforcement right away.** If too much time elapses between the behavior and the reinforcement, then you might be reinforcing something different. People react unconsciously to reinforcements. If Katie waits two hours before starting the conversation, then Joanne won't connect the reinforcement with the behavior.

- **You have to work hard, and it will take time.** Shaping can be time consuming. It requires you to be present and vigilant in looking for the current shaping behavior.

Shaping works best when you're trying to establish a new behavior that is, or at least can become, largely unconscious. Shaping works best with short, small behaviors that have a physiological basis.

 STRATEGIES

Strategy 48: When you can't reward a behavior because it doesn't exist, use shaping to kick-start the behavior.

Picking the Right Reward

One of the keys to Skinner's operant conditioning is that you have to pick the right reinforcement (reward). If Skinner used a penny as his reinforcement whenever a rat pressed a bar, he probably wouldn't have seen much bar pressing. Money is not a reinforcement for rats.

Rat food pellets are probably not an effective reinforcement for people. You have to pick a reinforcement that that particular person wants. It's sometimes tricky to find the right reinforcement.

For example, let's say you want your sales people to use the new Customer Relationship Manager (CRM) software you've purchased. You offer a trip to Las Vegas for each salesperson who uses the CRM software at least 30 times in the next 30 days.

What's wrong with this idea? It might work, but it might not. Here are some reasons why it might not work:

- In this case you're kind of using a fixed ratio schedule (after using the CRM 30 times, you get the reinforcement). I say "kind of" because you've added the 30-day stipulation. But you haven't done anything to establish the behavior. You'd be better off giving a small reinforcement every time each salesperson uses the CRM, and then follow up with the fixed ratio schedule as planned. The small reinforcement could be a leaderboard where people's names appear with the number of times they've used the CRM that week (the reinforcement is acknowledgement), or give praise when someone uses the CRM.

- A trip to Las Vegas might not be a reinforcement for a particular individual. Some of the salespeople might not like Las Vegas, or might feel that they've been doing too much travel and spent too much time away from their families. In these cases a trip to Las Vegas might not be an effective reinforcement.

Many things can be a reinforcement. Here are some examples (not all appropriate for the workplace):

> Money
> Food
> Tickets to concerts or sporting events
> Jewelry
> Clothes
> Praise
> Appreciation
> Autonomy
> Social interaction
> Sex

If the person wants it, then it's a reinforcement.

PROMISING MONETARY REWARDS RELEASES DOPAMINE

Brian Knutson (Knutson 2001) studied corporate pay incentive plans and found that when you promise people a monetary reward for their work, there is increased activity in the nucleus accumbens. This is the same area and same activity you see if people are anticipating cocaine, tobacco, or any addictive substance. Dopamine is released. Also, there's an increased tendency for risky behavior after the release of the dopamine and increased activity in the nucleus accumbens (the same reaction occurs after anticipating other addictive substances).

 STRATEGIES

Strategy 49: Choose a reward that the person really wants. Otherwise, rewards don't work.

When to Give the Reward

Once you decide on the reward and schedule (continuous, variable, and so on) you're going to use, make sure that you give the reward right away. For the reward to have the maximum effect on behavior, people have to be able to connect the reward to the actual behavior they performed.

For example, let's say you're using continuous reinforcement to establish a new behavior for someone on your team. Every time he comes to a meeting on time, you praise him, "Thanks, Jim, for being early to the meeting."

You need to say that to him as he walks into the room. If you wait a couple days and say, "It was great that you came to Monday's meeting on time," then the effect of the praise will be lessened.

And certainly don't give a reward ahead of time for behavior you are hoping to see ("I'll give you the raise but I expect you to meet your deadlines going forward"). Rewards are effective only if they come *after* the desired behavior is performed.

 STRATEGIES

Strategy 50: When you provide rewards, give them immediately after the behavior (according to the schedule you're using).

Strategy 51: When you provide rewards, give them *after* the behavior, not *before* the behavior.

Negative Reinforcement

So far all of our examples have been about positive reinforcement. We've used examples of giving people things they want, and then the behavior increases:

BEHAVIOR		REINFORCEMENT		MORE OF THAT BEHAVIOR
Turn the report in on time	→	Get praise: "Great job meeting that deadline!"	→	Submit more reports on time
Get an A	→	Get $5	→	Get more A's

We haven't talked yet about negative reinforcement. People often confuse negative reinforcement with punishment, but they are not at all the same thing. Negative reinforcement is powerful in changing behavior, and punishment is not as effective.

Let's start again with the rats and then move on to humans. You put a rat in a cage and give him an electrical shock. You teach the rat that he can press the bar and stop the shock. The shock is a negative reinforcement.

It's a reinforcement because using it results in an *increase* of the behavior. It's negative because the rat is pressing the bar (engaging in the behavior) to make the shock go away:

		MORE OF
BEHAVIOR	→ REINFORCEMENT →	THAT BEHAVIOR

Press the bar → *Shock goes away* → *More bar pressing*

Now let's try a human example. Joe wants to get his employee, Kevin, to keep his work area neater.

		MORE OF
BEHAVIOR	→ REINFORCEMENT →	THAT BEHAVIOR

Straighten up → *Reinforcement* → *Straighten up*
work area   *work area again*

Joe tries positive reinforcement first. He decides that every time Kevin straightens up his work area, he'll say something like, "Kevin, it's great to see your work area so clean!"

Straighten up work area → *Get praise* → *Straighten up work area more*

But it doesn't work. Kevin isn't cleaning up his work area. Joe thinks that part of the problem is that praise isn't an effective reinforcement for Kevin. Kevin doesn't care about getting praise, at least not from Joe.

Instead of looking for a different positive reinforcement, Joe decides to try negative reinforcement. Joe knows that Kevin doesn't like Joe to hang around, look over his shoulder, and tell him what to do. If Joe starts hanging around Kevin's work area, and starts nagging him about cleaning it up, he believes that will be negative reinforcement.

Joe thinks that if he uses that negative reinforcement, Kevin will clean up his work area more regularly:

BEHAVIOR		REINFORCEMENT		MORE OF THAT BEHAVIOR
Straighten up work area	→	Reinforcement (Joe stops hanging around and bugging Kevin)	→	Straighten up work area again

In negative reinforcement a behavior becomes stronger as a consequence of stopping or avoiding something the person doesn't like. Just like positive reinforcement, you have to figure out what it is that the particular individual would like to stop happening.

Negative reinforcement is why Skinner didn't like to use the term "reward." Reward implies that you are giving someone something that they want. By using the term "reinforcement," Skinner could talk about using anything to increase a behavior. Reinforcement is a more neutral term that includes the possibility of negative reinforcement, too.

 STRATEGIES

Strategy 52: You can use negative reinforcement to get people to do stuff. Figure out what someone *doesn't* want and remove it for them as a type of "reward."

Punishment

So what about punishment? Is that the same? Different? More effective? Less effective?

So far we've looked at applying something someone wants (positive reinforcement) and taking away something someone doesn't want (negative reinforcement). Punishment is different from both positive and negative reinforcement because when you punish someone you want a behavior to *decrease.*

You're not trying to *increase* a behavior (which is the case with both positive and negative reinforcement). Instead you're trying to *decrease* a behavior by applying something the person doesn't want.

PUNISHMENT CAN BACKFIRE

Applying a punishment can even backfire. In his book *Drive* (Pink 2009), Daniel Pink describes research by Gneezy (Gneezy 2000) where applying a penalty actually resulted in more of the unwanted behavior.

A daycare center decided to punish parents who showed up late to get their children by applying a monetary penalty. If the parents came late they were assessed a certain amount for each minute they were late. The hope was that by applying the punishment, parents would start coming on time.

But the opposite happened. When the penalty was applied the number of late pick-ups significantly increased. The reason is that the relationship changed. Before, when parents came late it was a matter of inconveniencing the daycare staff: "If I show up late then the staff can't go home on time." But when it became a purely monetary transaction (show up late = pay more money), then the parents didn't feel so bad in coming late. They were willing to pay the extra money.

Punishment can work, but it's less effective than either positive or negative reinforcement. It's more work to get people to *stop* doing something than to find an alternative behavior and get them to *do* the alternative behavior.

While reinforcement can result in strong and lasting behavior, punishment tends to work only as long as the punishment is applied. If you stop punishing the behavior, it comes right back.

 STRATEGIES

Strategy 53: Reward the behavior you want and ignore the behavior you don't want. Punishment is less effective than rewards.

Instincts

IMAGINE THAT YOU'RE walking down a path through the woods and suddenly you think you see a snake on the ground in front of you. You jump back in fear, your heart pounding. Your response is strong and automatic. Your survival instincts have kicked in.

We are constantly scanning our surroundings, alert for danger. That's one of our instincts—to survive. Our instincts include our reactions to novelty, danger, food, and sex. Instinctual responses are strong, fast, and largely unconscious.

Our instincts make us pay attention to certain things in our surroundings and ignore others. Not only that, most of our decisions are either made by, or at least greatly influenced by, our unconscious, instinctual reactions.

When you understand that many of our reactions and decisions come from instinct, you can use that knowledge to get people to do stuff.

Fear, Attention, and Memory

Because the old brain is on the alert for danger, fear is a powerful motivator for action. The unconscious detects and reacts to fear long before the conscious mind figures out what is going on. People have opinions based on fear. They will take actions based on fear. The drive to avoid something fearful is powerful.

Does this mean I'm suggesting that you scare people into doing what you want them to do? Not entirely. If you scare people too much, they'll avoid interacting with you. But small doses of fear will grab attention and motivate people to take action.

Mentioning in words or presenting a picture or video that shows someone's life in peril will grab attention. This includes accidents, severe weather (hurricanes, tornadoes, earthquakes), and wild animals.

You might not want your idea or your organization's brand to be associated with these negative messages and images, but some organizations and campaigns can make use of them to grab and focus attention.

For example, if an insurance company uses a picture of the aftermath of a huge storm in an ad to sell flood insurance, it will be able to grab attention because the picture shows devastation and our unconscious will pay attention to these messages of fear and danger.

Since a major job of our instincts is to keep us from harm, anything threatening our survival will get our attention. The threat doesn't have to be directed at us. Even watching a movie or an ad of someone *else* in danger will set off all our internal alarm bells. So if we're watching a scary car chase in a movie, our instincts are yelling, "Be careful, be careful!"

When our instincts sound an alarm, all of our information processing and emotional processing systems are on high alert and highly functioning. This means that anything that happens while we're on high alert will be processed deeply, and emotionally, in our memory. There's an entire branch of marketing now focused on activating our instincts and feeding us product information.

How can you use this to get people to do stuff? Say, for example, that a television commercial shows a dangerous situation (for example, a car chase) that culminates with someone receiving a particular brand of soda or a particular credit card. The idea is that all our systems are on heightened alert, so we'll remember the product and attach strong emotions to it.

In terms of attention getting and deep encoding in memory, it actually doesn't matter if we're scared or exhilarated; it doesn't matter if the emotions we're feeling are "positive" or "negative." What matters is that all our systems are on high alert.

STRATEGIES

Strategy 54: To grab attention, use messages and photos of dangerous events.

Strategy 55: To get people to remember you, your brand, or your message, use photos or wording that inspire fear.

Fear of Illness and Death

Jill is the communications director at a local hospital. She is starting an ad campaign to encourage people over age 50 to get regular checkups, take their medication, and undergo the preventive screenings recommended for people during midlife.

Jill contacts two agencies and asks for their ideas on a campaign. The two agencies give her very different advice about the ad campaign:

- Agency A puts together a communications campaign based on the theme of "Be the best you can be." It's all about staying healthy, being fit, and enjoying your friends, family, and favorite activities for the rest of your life. It includes pictures of active, fit, attractive people in their 50s and 60s.
- Agency B puts together a communications campaign based on the theme of "You can never be too careful." It's all about avoiding illness and chronic disease. This campaign has some pictures of active, fit, attractive people in their 50s and 60s, but it has more of people who are sick and dying.

Which campaign should Jill go with? It depends on what her goals are. If she wants to establish the hospital's brand as positive and healthy, then she should go with Agency A's "Be the best you can be." But if her goal is to get people to go see their doctor, get regular checkups, take their medication, and undergo preventive screenings, then Agency B's "You can never be too careful" is the campaign to go with. It will result in more immediate action.

People will be more likely to make a clinic appointment after being shown the messaging about fear of illness and death.

STRATEGIES

Strategy 56: To get people to take immediate action, use messages of fear and death.

Fear of Loss

One way you can get people to do stuff is to invoke a fear of loss. Our instincts are so alert and averse to loss of any kind that we are unconsciously more motivated to take action based on the fear of loss than on the anticipation of gain.

In a research study by Antoine Bechara (Bechara 1997), participants played a gambling game with decks of cards. Each person received $2,000 of pretend money. They were told that the goal was to lose as little of the $2,000 as possible, and to try to make as much over the $2,000 as they could.

Participants were asked to turn over a card from any of the four decks on the table, one card at a time. They continued turning over a card from the deck of their choice until the experimenter told them to stop. They didn't know when the game would end. Participants were told that every time they turned over a card, they earned money. They were also told that sometimes when they turned over a card, they earned money but also *lost* money (by paying it to the experimenter).

The participants didn't know any of the rules of the gambling game, but here are what the rules actually were:

- If they turned over any card in decks A or B, they earned $100. If they turned over any card in decks C or D, they earned $50.
- Some cards in decks A and B also required participants to pay the experimenter a lot of money, sometimes as much as $1,250. Some cards in decks C and D also required participants to pay the experimenter, but the amount they had to pay was only an average of $100.
- Over the course of the game, decks A and B produced net losses if participants continued using them. Continued use of decks C and D rewarded participants with net gains.

The rules of the game never changed. Although participants didn't know this, the game ended after 100 cards had been "played" (turned over).

Most participants started by trying all four decks. At first, they gravitated toward decks A and B because those decks paid out $100 per turn. But after about 30 turns, most turned to decks C and D. They then continued turning cards in decks C and D until the game ended.

During the study, the experimenter stopped the game several times to ask participants about the decks. The participants were connected to a skin conductance sensor to measure their SCR (skin conductance response). Their SCR readings were elevated when they played decks A and B (the "dangerous" decks) long before participants were conscious that A and B were dangerous.

When the participants played decks A and B, their SCRs increased even before they touched the cards in the decks. Their SCRs increased when they *thought* about using decks A and B. Instinctively they knew that decks A and B were dangerous and resulted in a loss. This showed up as a spike in the SCR. However, that was all unconscious. Their conscious minds didn't yet know that anything was wrong.

Eventually participants said they had a "hunch" that decks C and D were better, but the SCR showed that the old brain figured this out long before the new brain "got" it.

By the end of the game, most participants had more than a hunch and could articulate the difference in the two decks, but a full 30 percent of the participants couldn't explain why they preferred decks C and D. They said they just thought those decks were better.

People respond and react to unconscious signals of danger. The unconscious acts more quickly than the conscious mind. This means that people often cannot explain why they take the actions they do, or have the preferences they do.

Don't Make Me Lose It!

Barry Schwartz (Schwartz 2005) researched people buying cars. Participants test-drove cars with all the options.

- In one condition, they were shown the price of the car with all the options. If they said the price was too expensive, they were asked to take away the options in an effort to reduce the price.
- In another condition, they were shown the base price of the car (without options) along with the description and price of each option. They were asked to select which options they wanted to add, increasing the price with each option.

Participants spent more money in the first condition. Having experienced the car in its entirety, they were reluctant to lose what they, in some sense, felt they already had.

Is It 90 Percent Good or 10 Percent Bad?

In *Descartes' Error* (Damasio 1994), Antonio Damasio points out that we have such an automatic fear of losing that even the way things are phrased can be important.

He cites research in the medical field showing that when patients are told, "If you undergo this medical treatment, you have a 90 percent chance of living," patients choose the treatment.

If, however, patients are told, "If you undergo this medical treatment, you have a 10 percent chance of dying," patients are much less likely to choose the treatment.

STRATEGIES

Strategy 57: Understand that people are more motivated by the possibility of loss than the possibility of gain.

Strategy 58: Don't rely on people to self-report why they prefer one choice over another.

Strategy 59: When you want people to crave something, let them try it first. Once they've tried it, they won't want to lose it.

Quantities Are Limited

How many times have you received an offer to attend a event that says, "Seats are limited to 50. Sign up now to make sure you get a spot."

Why do people do that? Because it works! If something seems like it's scarce, or that it might become scarce, then both the value of the item and our desire for it increase. We're afraid of losing the opportunity to have or buy anything that's deemed scarce.

Stephen Worchel (Worchel 1975) asked people to rate chocolate chip cookies. Researchers put 10 cookies in one jar and 2 of the exact same cookies in another jar. The cookies from the jar with fewer cookies were rated as tasting better, even though the cookies were exactly the same!

Not only that, if there were a lot of cookies in the jar, and then a short time later most of the cookies were gone, the cookies that were left received an even higher rating than cookies that were in a jar where the number of cookies didn't change.

This strategy to get people to take action works for all kinds of things. Here are some examples:

- Buy this shirt now because there are only two left in your size.
- Before you can use this new online service, you have to be invited by someone who is already a member.
- We allow only 30 people at a time. Apply (or wait) and we'll let you know when there is an opening.
- The tickets are on sale only through next Thursday.
- We are accepting only five volunteers this year.

A concept similar to scarcity is the idea that things that are more expensive—and therefore harder to get (scarce)—are of higher quality. We unconsciously tend to want what is expensive. We unconsciously equate expensive with "better."

 STRATEGIES

Strategy 60: When you want people to value your product or service, make it scarce or difficult to get.

When People Want Familiar Brands

It's Friday afternoon and your boss calls you into his office to say that he's not happy with your latest project report. You've told him repeatedly that the project was in trouble and asked for more staff to be assigned. You feel that all your warnings were ignored.

Now your boss is telling you that this work will reflect badly on you and you may even lose your job. On the way home you stop at the grocery store because you're out of cereal for your morning breakfast. You're sad and scared after the conversation with your boss. Will you buy the cereal you always buy, or will you try something new?

According to research by Marieke de Vries (De Vries 2007) of Radboud University Nijmegen in the Netherlands, you'll buy the familiar brand.

Research shows that we want what is familiar when we're sad or scared. We're willing to try something new and different when we're feeling happy and not as sensitive to what is familiar.

This craving for the familiar and a preference for familiar brands may be tied to the basic fear of loss. When we're sad or scared, our instincts are on alert. We want to be safe, and a quick way to be safe is to go with what we know. A strong brand is familiar. A strong logo is familiar.

It's Easy to Change Someone's Mood

It turns out that it's remarkably easy to affect someone's mood, especially in the short term (for instance, during an hourlong presentation).

In Marieke de Vries's research, participants watched video clips of The Muppets (to instigate a good mood) versus clips from the movie *Schindler's List* (to instigate a bad mood). People reported their mood as significantly elevated after watching The Muppets and significantly lowered after *Schindler's List*. This mood change then affected their actions in the rest of the research study.

How can you apply these ideas, then, to get people to do stuff? Let's look at an example. Andrew is a sales rep for a company that sells computer and technology services. His company is making a lot of changes to their products and services. Andrew's job is to get his existing clients to try some of the new services.

Since he's asking people to try something new, he decides to get them into an upbeat mood and make them feel secure. He sits down in a one-on-one meeting with one of his clients. He first shows the client a video clip that his marketing department has put together for the new products and services. The video clip has upbeat music and positive messaging. After the video plays he instigates a discussion of all the "wins" that his client's company has had over the last year.

After setting the stage this way, he shares (in an upbeat way) what the new products and services are. He also includes the idea of scarcity to make the new products and services seem even more enticing. He tells his client that he has picked just a few special clients to try out the new services.

 STRATEGIES

Strategy 61: When you want people to try something new, engage them when they're in a good mood or help them get into a good mood by showing a fun or funny video.

Strategy 62: When you want people to try something new, make sure they're feeling safe and comfortable.

Strategy 63: When you want someone to stick with what's familiar, avoid putting them in a good mood.

Strategy 64: When you want people to stick with their usual choice and not try something new, use messaging that invokes the fear of loss.

We're Control Freaks

In *The Art of Choosing* (Iyengar 2010), Sheena Iyengar describes an experiment with rats. The rats were given a choice of a direct path to food or a path that had branches and therefore required choices to be made.

Both paths resulted in access to the same food in the same amounts. If all the rats wanted was food, then they should take the short, direct path. But the rats continuously preferred the path with branches.

In experiments with monkeys and pigeons, the animals learn to press buttons to get food. If given a choice between one button and multiple buttons, both monkeys and pigeons prefer multiple buttons.

In similar research with humans, people were given chips to use at a casino. They could use the chips at a table that had one roulette wheel, or at a table where they could choose from two roulette wheels. People preferred the table with two wheels, even though all the wheels were identical.

THE NEED TO CONTROL STARTS YOUNG

Sheena Iyengar describes a study of infants as young as four months old where the researchers attached the babies' hands to a string. The infants could move their hands to pull the string, which would cause music to play.

The researchers then detached the string from the music control. They played music at the same intervals, but the infants had no power over when the music played. The babies cried. They wanted to control when the music played.

Choices Mean Control and Control Means Survival

Even though it's not necessarily true, we equate having choices with having control. If we're to feel in control, we need to feel that our actions are powerful and that we have choices to make. Sometimes having many choices makes it harder to get what we want, but we still want the choices so we feel in control of the decision.

We have a desire to control our environment. This makes sense. Our instincts tell us that controlling the environment means an increase in the probability of survival. We need to feel that we're in control and that we have choices. If we have too many choices, we won't choose anything at all. But if we don't have any choices we lose motivation.

To get people to do stuff, you need to offer a few (three or four at most) clear choices so they feel in control. People won't always choose the fastest way to get something done. They might choose the way where they feel that they have some control.

When my two children were young, we used to have cleanup time on the weekends. Rather than assigning them household tasks to do, I made a list of all the possible chores that day, and awarded each task a number of points. The longer, more difficult, or undesirable tasks were given more points than the shorter, easier tasks.

I would then tell them how many points they had to achieve in tasks that day, and they could choose which ones to do. They felt they had some control over their work.

And I got help with the cleaning.

 STRATEGIES

Strategy 65: When you give people choices, you give them control—and people love to have control.

Strategy 66: Limit the number of choices to three or four. When you provide too many choices, people won't choose anything at all.

Safety and Participation

The best presentation I've ever been to was the performance by Bobby McFerrin. His concerts involve music and extensive audience interaction.

When I went to see him it was in a theater that seats 1,500 in a small city in Wisconsin. The theater was full, and the audience was appreciative, but reserved. But by the end of his 90-minute performance, he had the entire audience at the edge of their seats, ready to do anything he asked of them, including coming up on stage.

McFerrin is a masterful performer and a master at getting people to participate. He does this by bonding the group and taking it slow. You're sitting in a theater with a lot of strangers, and you don't want to look silly, but he gets you to first just make one small noise or sing one simple note. Everyone around you is doing it, so you do, too. He then builds on that one participation and asks for a little more and a little more, until everyone is freely participating.

> ▶ **NOTE** If you've never seen Bobby McFerrin engage audiences, check out
> this short, three-minute video: http://www.ted.com/talks/lang/en/bobby_
> mcferrin_hacks_your_brain_with_music.html

McFerrin is a master at making people feel safe. He never ridicules or
makes fun of anyone. His body language and comments make everyone feel
that they're doing great, doing exactly what he expects and knows they can
do. It feels safe to participate.

If you're going to ask people to participate in an activity (for example,
taking part in a discussion during a presentation or giving you feedback on
your website), start slow and make sure they feel safe. Have them do one
small activity before an activity that takes longer or is more complicated. You
can use humor to make people feel relaxed, but don't make fun of people as
a form of humor or they'll start to feel unsafe.

STRATEGIES

Strategy 67: When you want people to participate, make them feel safe.

New and Improved!

Because our instincts are always on alert for threats and dangers, we're pre-
disposed to be wary of change. Novelty gets our attention. We tend to ignore
what's the same, and pay attention to what's new. It's efficient—we'll stay safe
if some part of our unconscious spends more time and attention noticing
what's changed and ignores what hasn't.

This attention to novelty and change is one of the reasons why we get
"addicted" to our technological devices. They instantly let us know when there's
a new message, but the notices are unpredictable. We don't know when they'll
occur. That means our attention is drawn over and over again to the device
as soon as we see or hear an alert.

The first hurdle in getting people to do something is to get their attention. If you do something new or different, show an unexpected image, or
surprise them in any way, you'll grab their attention.

STRATEGIES

Strategy 68: To grab attention, use novelty. Once you have people's attention, give them your message.

Keep 'Em Comin' Back for More

One of the most important neurotransmitters in our brains is dopamine. Neuroscientists have been studying what they call the dopamine system since 1958, when it was identified by Arvid Carlsson and Nils-Ake Hillarp at the National Heart Institute of Sweden. Dopamine is created in various parts of the brain and is critical in all sorts of brain functions, including thinking, moving, sleeping, mood, attention, motivation, seeking, and reward.

The latest thinking on dopamine is that it's not just the "pleasure" chemical in the brain. Dopamine actually causes us to want, desire, seek out, and search. It increases our general level of arousal, motivation, and goal-directed behavior.

Dopamine makes us curious about ideas and fuels our search for information. It is the opioid system, more than the dopamine system, that's involved in feelings of pleasure.

According to Kent Berridge (Berridge 1998), these "wanting" (dopamine) and "liking" (opioid) systems are complementary. The wanting system propels us to action and the liking system makes us feel satisfied, and therefore makes us pause our seeking. If our seeking isn't turned off, then we start to run in an endless loop. The dopamine system is stronger than the opioid system. We seek more than we are satisfied.

Dopamine is critical from an evolutionary standpoint. If humans had not been driven by curiosity to seek out new things and ideas, then they would have just sat in their caves. The dopamine seeking system kept our ancestors motivated to move through the world, learn, and survive.

Seeking was more likely to keep humans alive than sitting around in a satisfied stupor. Research on rats shows that if you destroy dopamine neurons, rats can walk, chew, and swallow, but they will starve to death even when food is right next to them. They have lost the desire to go get the food.

You can use this desire for information to get people to do stuff by stimulating information-seeking behavior.

Addicted to More

The dopamine system is most powerfully stimulated when it gets a little bit of information at a time. After we consume a little bit of information, then dopamine is released and makes us want more.

How can you use the dopamine system to encourage people to consume more information? Let's start with an example.

Jesse works in the human resources department of a large company. He's developed a video course on how to resolve conflict, and ensured that the videos are interesting, well produced, and of high quality. He wants the employees at the company to take the whole video course. What should he do to increase the likelihood of people taking the entire course?

a.   Break up the course into small lessons of a few minutes each and package them so people are accessing only a few lessons at a time.

b.   Present the course as a single, 90-minute video.

Jesse should use option a. By breaking up the lessons and making only a few available at a time, he'll stimulate the employees' dopamine system and they'll want to continue on to the next lesson. People are more likely to take the course and be motivated to finish if Jesse provides the sections one at a time. This will maintain the desire for more information.

 STRATEGIES

Strategy 69: Influence people to desire more by giving them a limited amount of information.

Novelty and Dopamine

You can also combine novelty and information seeking to get people to do stuff. Dopamine is stimulated by unpredictability: when something unexpected happens, it stimulates the dopamine system.

Think about electronic devices, for example. Messages show up, but you don't know exactly when they'll arrive or whom they'll be from. It's unpredictable. This is exactly what stimulates the dopamine system.

Having information show up unexpectedly with an auditory or visual alert makes people want to engage in the behavior (for example, checking for messages again and again).

The dopamine system is especially sensitive to cues that a reward is coming. If there is a small, specific cue that signifies that something is going to happen, that sets off your dopamine system. Our instincts are constantly on the alert for anything new or novel.

In Chapter 5, "Carrots and Sticks," we showed that the brain is easily conditioned to respond to a particular stimulus. When you pair a stimulus such as a beep, tone, or visual alert with new information or a new message, the response becomes automatic and instinctual. You can't avoid paying attention.

STRATEGIES

Strategy 70: When you want undivided attention, make the stimulus unpredictable and include an auditory or visual alert.

Food and Sex

In this chapter we've talked about unconscious reactions to novelty, fear, and the desire for control. There are two other instinctual drives that are critical in grabbing attention and making decisions: food and sex.

Use Food to Motivate

Our unconscious knows that we need food to survive. The sight or smell of food grabs our attention. Depending on how hungry we are, food might be a temporary distraction or an overwhelming urge. We pay attention to food.

The real thing is the most attention getting, but even a photograph of food will make us sit up and take notice. The food needs to be front and center, however. Showing a picture of people sitting at a restaurant implies food, but to capture the instinctual attention, the food must be very obvious.

Imply Sex

We all know that sex, or the implication of sex, is a powerful attention getter. The desire for sex is one of our strongest instincts. Even the subtlest hints of sex—a certain look to the eyes, a flash of skin—are powerful enough to engage our attention.

In addition to attention getting, we often make decisions, largely unconscious, based on the possibility of sex. We decide to purchase a particular product or service because an advertisement contains the idea that by using the product we will have more sex or be more sexually attractive to others.

STRATEGIES

Strategy 71: To grab attention, use actual food, the smell of food, or even a picture of food.

Strategy 72: To grab attention and affect decision making, use any hint of sex—as long as the use of sex is appropriate.

The Desire
for Mastery

IF YOU WANT TO UNDERSTAND the importance of mastery, spend an hour watching a one-year-old. Watch him try to stand up on his own or walk. Watch him play with a puzzle or any other toy. All people—children and adults—have a desire for mastery. It's a universal human drive to want to master a skill or our environment. People are driven to master a sport, a video game, or skills such as welding, performing surgery, or playing the piano.

The wonderful thing about using the drive for mastery to motivate people to do stuff is that this drive is wired into each of us, and it's easy to stimulate the desire. But the tricky thing is that the motivation has to be intrinsic, that is, internal to the person. You can't make someone want to master a particular skill. In order for mastery to be a powerful force, the drive must come from that individual. Luckily it's possible to influence the environment and the situation so the innate desire for mastery emerges.

Here's a psychologist's definition of mastery from George Morgan (Morgan 1990):

> Mastery motivation is a psychological force that stimulates an individual to attempt independently, in a focused and consistent manner, to solve a problem or master a skill or task which is at least moderately challenging for him or her.

Humans are naturally curious and this curiosity helps us master our environment. The more time children spend mastering their environment, the more successful they are at thinking and learning as an adult.

What happens when children or adults try to master something? They pay attention, focus their concentration, and acquire information. Because this is a basic drive, you can use the desire for mastery to get people to do stuff.

Mastery Trumps Rewards

You've purchased some new technology for your designers, and you want them to learn new skills so that they can make the best possible use of it. You believe that this new way of working will save significant time and money, and result in better designs. But you also know that the learning curve is relatively high.

The management team has suggested that you reward the designers by giving a cash bonus to any of them who create a design using the new technology and the new process. Should you give a cash bonus?

Before we answer that question, let's look back at some research from 1973:

Marianne is an art teacher at an elementary school. She wants to encourage her students to spend more time practicing their drawing. She creates a "Good Drawing Certificate" to give to her students.

If her goal is to have her students spend more time drawing, and to want to draw more over time, how should she give them the certificate? Should she give them one every time they draw, or only sometimes?

Mark Lepper (Lepper 1973) conducted research on this question. He divided the children into three groups:

- Group 1 was the "expected" group: The researchers showed the children the "Good Drawing Certificate" and asked if they wanted to draw in order to get the certificate.
- Group 2 was the "unexpected" group: The researchers asked the children if they wanted to draw, but didn't mention anything about a certificate. After the children spent time drawing, they received an unexpected drawing certificate.
- Group 3 was the control group: The researchers asked the children if they wanted to draw, but didn't mention a certificate and didn't give them one.

The real part of the experiment came two weeks later. During playtime, the drawing tools were put out in the room. The children weren't asked about drawing, the tools were just made available in the room. So what happened?

Children in Groups 2 (unexpected) and 3 (control) spent the most time drawing. The children in Group 1, those who received an expected reward, spent the least time drawing.

"Contingent" rewards (rewards given based on specific behavior that is spelled out ahead of time) resulted in less of the desired behavior. Later the researchers went on to do more studies like this, with adults as well as children, and found similar results.

When Rewards Backfire

Let's go back to the question about whether you should give cash for designers who use the new technology.

The answer is that it would be better to stimulate a desire for mastery than to give cash. It's not actually the money that dampens the desire for mastery. It's the contingency aspect of the bonus.

If you give the designers a cash bonus when they're not expecting one, that won't necessarily kill the desire to master the technology. But if you tell them that they'll get a cash bonus every time they use the new technology, that *will* dampen their desire for mastery. The difference is the contingency.

In the first case the designers weren't expecting a reward. In the second they were, and the behavior (use of the new processes and technology) is required in order to get the reward.

Research on mastery shows that if you give a cash bonus that's contingent on use, there will be an initial uptick in trying out the new technology. But that will wane. You need to engage the drive for mastery if you want the designers to embrace the new technology and use it on an ongoing basis.

Instead of offering a cash bonus each time the designers do things the new way, it would be better to engage their curiosity about the new technology. Let them know that these are important new skill sets that will serve them for the rest of their careers.

Carrots and Sticks versus Mastery

In Chapter 5, "Carrots and Sticks," we talked about how to use reinforcements to get people to do stuff. Now we're saying that's a bad idea, and that you should use mastery instead. So, what gives?

The best, although complicated, answer is that, in general, mastery is a better strategy because it uses intrinsic motivation, and, in general, intrinsic motivation works better over the long haul.

However, there are many situations in which reinforcements are powerful. If people don't have intrinsic motivation to do a task, and if it will be hard to get them to apply intrinsic motivation, then reinforcements work well.

Routine Tasks versus Complicated Tasks

Another distinction is what kind of task you want people to do. If you want them to do a routine task that doesn't require a lot of thinking, for example, keep their work space organized and clean, then reinforcements will work as well as, or even better and faster than, mastery.

Mastery implies that there is a skill or knowledge to learn. In a routine task there's a limit to how much mastery is really involved. Without the sense of mastering a challenging skill or developing a new body of knowledge, it's hard to get intrinsic motivation going. So there's still a place for using carrots and sticks.

STRATEGIES

Strategy 73: When you want people to do something complicated, something that requires learning new skills or gaining a new body of knowledge, use the desire for mastery. If not, then reinforcements may be the better option.

Strategy 74: When you want to get people to do stuff over the long term, engage their desire for mastery—don't just give them cash or other rewards.

Make People Feel Special

If you're going to stimulate the desire for mastery, then you have to make people feel that they're really mastering a new and important skill.

Have you ever read Mark Twain's *The Adventures of Tom Sawyer*? Tom has been told to paint a white fence in front of his aunt's house. He wants to get out of the chore, and tries to figure out how to get someone else to do it.

Tom decides to pretend that painting the fence is a special activity that only the skilled can do. When other boys come by, they get the message from Tom that painting the fence is a special and challenging activity. They want to paint the fence too, but Tom is hesitant. He tells them,

> "I reckon there ain't one boy in a thousand, maybe two thousand, that can do it the way it's got to be done."

I'm not suggesting that you be as deceptive as Tom Sawyer was. But people do like to feel that they're part of an elite group. We like to feel that we have special talents and skills that set us apart. If you indicate that a particular task requires special talents, skills, or knowledge, then people are more likely to want to do it. You will stimulate the desire for mastery.

STRATEGIES

Strategy 75: When you make people feel that only members of an elite group can do a certain task, they'll be more motivated to master the task.

Challenge Is Motivating

Mastery is not just about feeling special. We like challenges. Challenges motivate us.

Mark Twain captures this in that same passage from *The Adventures of Tom Sawyer:*

He had discovered a great law of human action, without knowing it—namely, that in order to make a man or a boy covet a thing, it is only necessary to make the thing difficult to attain.

When something is hard to achieve, when it is challenging, people want to do it. Making a task challenging is another way to energize the desire for mastery. If you make it too easy, then the desire for mastery won't be stimulated. Of course, if you make it *too* challenging then it will seem impossible, and the desire for mastery will be quashed.

You have to find the right amount of challenge for the people you're trying to motivate. This sometimes comes down to finding the right amount of challenge for a particular individual at a particular moment.

For example, several years ago my husband suggested that I learn to play jazz piano. He was learning jazz guitar, and he thought that if I learned piano we could then play together. I've played a little bit of piano over the years, but never much, and certainly never jazz.

The idea of mastering jazz piano was appealing, and it certainly was a challenge. So I started. I attended some jazz workshops, tried to find a piano teacher that could teach me jazz, and bought instructional books and audio courses. The idea of the challenge was motivating.

But the challenge proved to be too much. I learned a lot about jazz and music theory. I mastered some of the fundamentals of jazz, jazz theory, and even some fundamentals about piano. I reached a point, however, where going beyond a few fundamentals seemed daunting. I didn't feel that I'd be able to achieve a level of mastery that would allow me to comfortably sit in and play tunes with other amateurs.

When we don't feel that we're making progress, and when we don't feel that we can achieve at least some level of mastery, then challenge is not motivating anymore.

What I did instead was switch to jazz singing. I thought that, for me, singing jazz would be something I could achieve a more passable level at than playing jazz piano. I'm not saying that mastering jazz vocals is inherently easier than mastering jazz piano. But for me the challenge of learning to sing jazz was the right amount of challenge. I felt it was challenging, but that I could get to a passable level of proficiency. I was motivated by that desire for mastery. It proved to be the right level of challenge, and many years later I'm still learning and challenging myself with singing jazz. I enjoy the challenge and I enjoy the level of mastery I've been able to achieve. I'm no Ella Fitzgerald, Janet Planet, or Diana Krall, but I'm able to sit in with other amateurs and sing a jazz tune.

If I'd found the right teacher to work with on a regular basis from the start, I might have stuck with jazz piano. A good teacher knows how to take a body of knowledge or skill set and break it down into smaller chunks. A good teacher is a master of mastery. Knowing how to chunk skills and information into the right-size bites for a particular individual is what a good teacher does. And that's the key to motivating people with mastery. You need to find the right amount of challenge to spark the desire for mastery, but not overwhelm it.

STRATEGIES

Strategy 76: When you make a task seem challenging (but not impossible), people will be motivated to pursue it.

Autonomy Encourages Mastery

Since the desire for mastery is an intrinsic motivation, this means the individual has to set the goal and decide on the pace of achievement. Autonomy, or the ability to govern oneself and one's work, is important to mastery.

We like to do things the way we want to do them, and when we want to do them. We like autonomy. Autonomy motivates us because it makes us feel in control.

For example, Curtis manages a team of programmers. He'd like his team to become skilled with some new programming technology. Instead of telling his team how to learn the skill, which training course to attend, and so on, Curtis will better stimulate the desire for mastery if he points his staff to some resources but lets them make the decisions. He might discuss options of how they can master the new skill, but if he lets them do the research on their own about how to learn the new skill, whether to take a course, what course to take, and when to take it, the autonomy will make them more motivated to learn the skill.

STRATEGIES

Strategy 77: When you provide people with autonomy, they feel a stronger desire for mastery and thus are more motivated.

When Struggling Is a Good Thing

If you grew up in Asia, then the idea of struggling as a good thing may strike you as common sense. But if you grew up the US or in other Western countries, then this idea may seem counterintuitive.

Many of us in the West assume that struggling is humiliating and will prevent people from being motivated. According to James Stigler from UCLA, Western cultures think that struggle shows that you're not smart enough; it's a sign of not having the ability to do the work.

In contrast, in many Asian cultures and classrooms, struggle is assumed to be something that everyone must go through in order to learn. Many Asian cultures see struggle as an opportunity, not a problem. It's seen as part of the learning process. And when you finally do break through to a resolution of a problem you've been struggling with, it shows that you have persistence.

Indeed, research shows that people learn from making mistakes. Mastery involves persisting in the face of struggle, and triumphing over the struggle to master the information.

Think about video games. If a video game is so easy that you seldom make a mistake, then the game won't be very interesting. Making mistakes and struggling to master the game are part of why the game is compelling and fun. That degree of challenge stimulates our desire to keep playing.

 STRATEGIES

Strategy 78: When you make people struggle, at least a little bit, it increases their sense of mastery and thereby increases their level of motivation.

Strategy 79: Provide people with opportunities to make mistakes.

Give Feedback to Keep Motivation Going

Along with allowing people to make mistakes, you can give them feedback on their mistakes to help them learn and adjust what they're doing. The right kind of feedback at the right time can increase the desire for mastery.

Use caution, however: the wrong type of feedback at the wrong time can hinder the desire for mastery. Valerie Shute (Shute 2007) analyzed hundreds of studies on feedback. Here are a few ideas to keep in mind if you want to use feedback to keep people motivated to continue the desire for mastery.

Correct or Not?

The first piece of information to give is whether someone is doing things correctly or not. Be very clear. It's all too easy to be vague.

Let's say that Jerome is training Kathleen, a new barista at the coffee shop he manages. Kathleen makes a practice cup of espresso, and Jerome says, "That's a good first try. But perhaps you can make it a little better." Is Jerome saying that Kathleen did it correctly or not? It's hard to tell from that statement. When you're giving feedback make sure it's clear.

Jerome could have said, "You didn't clean out the filter thoroughly enough. All the residue needs to be flushed out. Let's give that another try." Now Kathleen will have no doubt that what she did was not correct.

Provide a Short Elaboration

The previous feedback, "You didn't clean out the filter thoroughly enough. All the residue needs to be flushed out. Let's give that another try," includes what is called *elaboration*. If Jerome had only said, "You didn't clean out the filter thoroughly enough," then he'd be telling Kathleen that what she did was incorrect, but not giving an explanation. The short explanation ("All the residue needs to be flushed out") is the elaboration.

Providing elaboration gives Kathleen the details she needs to know to correct what she did wrong. Without elaboration, it would be hard for Kathleen to improve the next time she tries the task.

Elaboration should be short. What if Jerome's feedback was, "Every time that you brew an espresso you need to dump out the spent grounds, of course, and then rinse the filter with hot water. Make sure you check the filter basket for residue and make sure it's entirely clear before you replace it. Run water through the screen and scrub it with a brush. Don't forget to empty the drop tray several times a day, and you also have to wipe off the frothing wand after each cup."

This might be important information, but it's way too long as an elaboration for feedback on one step.

Decide on the Best Time for Feedback

You might think that giving feedback right away is the best thing, but that may not be the case. If a task involves several small steps, then it might be best to wait until the person has completed all the steps and then give feedback on the entire task.

If you give feedback on every little step, then you risk interrupting the normal flow of the task and you make it hard for the person to correct mistakes on her own. On the other hand, if you wait too long then she might not even remember what it was she did that you're giving feedback on.

A good rule of thumb is to break up the task into smaller steps. Give feedback when the person has completed three to four steps, or after the person has made two to three errors, whichever comes first.

Don't Combine Praise with Feedback

Keep feedback objective. Remember that mastery has to do with intrinsic motivation, not reinforcement. People don't need your praise to keep going, and switching to praise takes the focus off of intrinsic motivation and puts it on extrinsic motivation. This may actually decrease the desire for mastery.

Also, feedback is often about what needs to change. Combining feedback on what the person did incorrectly and what needs to change with praise is often confusing. For example, Jerome said to Kathleen, "You didn't clean out the filter thoroughly enough. All the residue needs to be flushed out. Let's give that another try."

His feedback was objective and did not include praise. What if Jerome had said, "You didn't clean out the filter thoroughly enough. All the residue needs to be flushed out. Great job, though, for your first time. You're really getting the hang of it! Let's give that another try."

The second way combines feedback and praise. It might make Jerome feel better, but it probably confuses Kathleen. Did she do the cleaning correctly or not?

Knowing when to give feedback is one of the distinguishing factors between a great teacher or mentor and a not-so-great teacher.

 STRATEGIES

Strategy 80: Give feedback to help people learn from their mistakes, but don't interrupt their work in order to do so.

Strategy 81: When you give feedback, provide a short elaboration.

Strategy 82: Pick the right time to give feedback.

Strategy 83: When you use feedback to increase the desire for mastery, keep the feedback objective and don't include praise.

Go with the Flow

Say you're totally engrossed in an activity, totally in the moment. Everything else falls away, your sense of time changes, and you almost forget who you are and where you are. This is called a flow state.

When you can encourage a flow state, you can get people to stay focused and do an activity at peak ability for a long time. When you encourage a flow state, you're encouraging the desire for mastery.

The Flow State

The man who wrote the book (literally) on flow is Mihaly Csikszentmihalyi (Csikszentmihalyi 2008). He's been studying the flow state around the world for many years. Let's look at some facts about the flow state, the conditions that make it occur, and what it feels like.

There Is Focused Attention on a Task

The ability to control and focus attention is critical. When we get distracted by anything outside of the activity we're engaged in, the flow state dissipates.

There Is a Specific, Clear, and Achievable Goal

No matter what the activity is, the flow state comes about when there is a specific goal. When we're intensely focused on a task, we let in only information that fits with the goal.

Research shows that we need to feel that we have a good chance of reaching the goal in order to get into, and hold onto, the flow state. If we think we have a good chance of *failing* at the goal, then the flow state will not be induced. Conversely, if the activity is not challenging enough, then it won't hold our attention and the flow state will end.

There Is Feedback

In order to stay in the flow state, we need feedback as to the achievement of the goal (see the previous section on the right type of feedback). Some of the most valuable feedback comes from the task itself.

For example, if I'm playing piano in a flow state, I'm getting constant feedback by listening to the sounds coming from the piano. I don't necessarily need feedback from a piano teacher all the time.

There Is Control

Control is an important condition for the flow state. We don't necessarily have to be in control, or even feel like we're in control of the entire situation, but we do have to feel that we're exercising significant control over our own actions in a challenging situation.

Time Changes

For some of us, time speeds up—we look up and hours have gone by. For others, time slows down.

The Self Does Not Feel Threatened

In order to enter a flow state, our sense of self and survival must not feel threatened. We have to be relaxed enough to engage all of our attention in the task at hand. In fact, most of us lose our sense of self when we're absorbed in a task.

The Flow State Is Personal

All of us have different activities that put us in a flow state. What triggers a flow state for you is different from others.

The Flow State Crosses Cultures

So far the flow state seems to be a common human experience, with the exception of people with some mental illnesses. Those who have schizophrenia, for example, have a hard time inducing or staying in a flow state, probably because they have a hard time with some of the other items above, such as focused attention, control, or the self not feeling threatened.

The Flow State Is Pleasurable

Simply put, we like being in the flow state.

The Prefrontal Cortex and Basal Ganglia Are Both Involved

The prefrontal cortex is responsible for focused attention, and the basal ganglia are involved in dopamine production, which produces the pleasurable feeling as well as the drive to keep going.

How to Encourage a Flow State

We can go into a flow state for a wide variety of tasks. For example, we can be in a flow state when we're playing a musical instrument, cooking a meal, writing a report, or giving a presentation. The flow state isn't limited to particular kinds of tasks. We don't have to be doing something creative in order to be in a flow state.

Flow states occur because of the *way* we're doing a task, not because of the type of task we are doing. When we're in a flow state, we're motivated to continue with what we're doing. We also want to do the task again in order to get back into a flow state.

Here's an example. Let's say you ask Jeff, one of the people on your team, to write a white paper on a particular topic. You want him to figure out what research he may need to do, whom he might need to interview, and so on. You want him to write the white paper and present a summary of it to the team. You want him to like doing this, because you'd like him to take the initiative in suggesting and writing additional white papers in the future.

Here are some ideas of how to encourage people to go into and stay in a flow state, using Jeff as an example:

- Give people a specific task to do, with an achievable goal.

    Tell Jeff what you want to accomplish: you want a white paper and a presentation for the team. Tell him that you know he hasn't done this kind of writing before, and that it might be challenging, but that you believe he's up to the task. Tell him specifics about the white paper, for example, the length, and when you want it done by.

- Let people have as much autonomy as possible, for example, how they do the task, where, when, and with whom.

    You can point Jeff to some initial resources, or tell him to come to you if he gets stuck, but let him know that it's up to him how he goes about doing his research.

- Don't interrupt them while they're doing the task.

    Refrain from asking Jeff whenever you see him how the white paper is coming along.

- Build in the opportunity for feedback, preferably from the task itself.

    Jeff can tell whether he's making progress on the white paper or not, so there's some feedback that will come while he's doing the task.

If you set up the task in this way, Jeff may go into a flow state while writing the white paper. If he does, he'll enjoy the task and be more motivated to keep at it and do more white papers in the future.

STRATEGIES

Strategy 84: When you induce a flow state, people will work longer and harder.

Strategy 85: To keep a flow state going, give people control over their actions during the activity.

Strategy 86: To keep a flow state going, don't interrupt people.

Strategy 87: To keep the flow state going, make sure the task is challenging but not impossible.

8

Tricks of the Mind

YOU'VE PROBABLY SEEN optical illusions like the one shown in **Figure 8.1.**

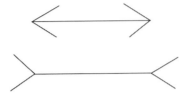

FIGURE 8.1 The Müller-Lyer illusion.

The line on the top looks shorter than the line on the bottom, but they are actually the same size. Just as we can fall prey to optical illusions, we can be taken in by cognitive illusions. Our brains can fool us into thinking that something is true when it isn't. If you understand these "tricks of the mind," then you can start to understand how people think, or more likely, how they aren't thinking, but rather reacting automatically. You can use these automatic thinking patterns to get people to do stuff.

Look at **Figure 8.2.**

FIGURE 8.2 What do you see?

What do you see? You can probably tell very quickly that you're looking at a photograph of a small boy, and that the boy looks sad. You did all that without really thinking. In his book *Thinking, Fast and Slow* (Kahneman 2011), Daniel Kahneman describes two different systems of how the brain thinks. He calls these System 1 and System 2, or "automatic" and "effortful" thinking. Interpreting the photo is an example of System 1 thinking. It's quick, intuitive, and automatic. We've talked in previous chapters about the idea that most mental processing occurs unconsciously. Much of what Kahneman is describing as System 1 thinking occurs unconsciously.

Now look at the following math problem and see if you can work out the answer in your head, without using paper and pen. Really, stop reading and try to work out the answer in your head at least for 30 seconds.

$18 \times 26 = ?$

I hope you really tried, but I'm willing to bet you didn't finish the task. You probably gave up. This is an example of System 2 thinking. It's hard. It takes effort. It's not automatic. It requires conscious thought as well as effort. Kahneman describes the research that shows that as we work hard at a System 2 task, our pupils dilate. You can tell when people are engaged in System 2 thinking if you look closely at their eyes.

Let's try one more. Here's a word problem:

A bat and a ball cost $1.10. The bat costs $1.00 more than the ball. How much does the ball cost?

What did you answer? This question is part of a series of questions from the "Cognitive Reflection Test" developed by Shane Frederick (Frederick 2005). You would think that this question would stimulate System 2 thinking. It's a mathematical question, after all. Interestingly, most people initially give the answer that the ball costs $.10. But that's a wrong answer. The answer is $.05. (If the ball costs $.05 and the bat is $1.00 more, then the bat is $1.05. $1.05 plus $.05 equals a total of $1.10.)

System 1 almost always jumps in first to try to answer every question, solve every problem, and react to whatever is going on. When we look at the bat and ball question, System 1 gives the intuitive answer of $.05 and then we think we are done. System 2 didn't even kick in.

Your Lazy Brain

System 1 almost always trumps System 2. Basically our brains are lazy. They don't want to work hard.

From a biological and evolutionary viewpoint, thinking hard uses up a lot of glucose, which means that we'll have to go searching for food. While we're doing effortful thinking about where to go look for food, we might not notice that a lion is headed our way. Much of the time our brains will take the easy, automatic System 1 answer. It's safer and easier to stick with System 1 answers most of the time.

We have evolved to let our System 1 (intuitive and quick) brain processes make most of the decisions and come up with "best guess" answers. Most of the time, even the hardworking, hard-thinking System 2 will go along with the answers that System 1 comes up with. It can be really hard to get System 2 to override. Let's review the Müller-Lyer lines from the beginning of this chapter (**Figure 8.3**).

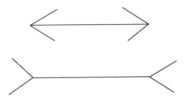

FIGURE 8.3 The Müller-Lyer illusion.

You now know that the lines are the same size. In fact, I invite you to go get a ruler and verify that they're the same size. But it doesn't matter. No matter how many times you look at the lines, no matter whether you believe me or whether you get the ruler and measure, you'll still see one line as longer than the other. No matter how much your System 2 thinking proves to you that they're the same length or explains why one looks longer than the other, your System 1 thinking will still see one as longer than the other and will send that message to System 2.

But what does this have to do with getting people to do stuff?

Most of the time our reliance on System 1 thinking serves us well. It keeps us alive, enables us to deal with large amounts of data coming at us, and makes sense of the world. But sometimes this System 1 thinking makes quick decisions without thinking things through enough. You can use this tendency to make quick, snap decisions to get people to do stuff.

If you understand the difference between System 1 and System 2 thinking you can either a) make your request/task/argument in a way that makes sense to System 1, and therefore greatly increases your chance of a quick "OK!" response, or b) you can do a few very specific things to wake up System 2 in case you need the person to think carefully before making a decision or taking an action.

In order to get people to do stuff, you need to decide which system you want to activate, and then take steps to activate it. Otherwise System 1 will triumph.

STRATEGIES

Strategy 88: When you want people to make a quick decision, make the thinking easy for them.

Strategy 89: When you want people to think things through, make the thinking more difficult for them.

Looking for Blame

"Tim had an argument with his brother. The next day he showed up at school with bruises all over his body."

As you read the above sentences, chances are that you automatically and intuitively applied causation to the sentences: Tim has bruises because he had an argument with his brother, right? The "story" doesn't say that explicitly, but your System 1 thinking will jump to that conclusion. Of course, Tim might have had only a verbal argument with his brother, and later that day played a rough game of football with friends that resulted in his bruises.

System 1 applies causation (whether it exists or not) because it likes a tidy story. System 1 likes everything to tie together in a neat package. It likes coherence. When ideas and facts "cohere" or go together, then System 1 can make those quick connections and decisions.

Scientists and researchers dislike this tendency for people to apply causation where it may not exist. They call this a logical fallacy. Two common logical fallacies are

1. Two events that occur together are assumed to have a cause-and-effect relationship.
2. If one event follows another, the first event caused the second.

Perhaps you've heard the phrase "correlation does not imply causation." Different factors are often associated together, but it may be hard or impossible to know which causes which.

For example, data from several research studies showed that women who took hormone replacement therapy also had a lower incidence of heart disease.

Doctors assumed, therefore, that the hormone replacement therapy would protect women from heart disease, and many began to prescribe it to their female patients who were going through menopause. But the initial studies were reporting a *correlation* between these two factors, not a causative relationship.

It turns out that if you give these hormones to women in general, it actually increases heart disease! The relationship between hormones and heart disease in the earlier studies was actually a relationship between socioeconomic status and heart disease.

The women who were asking for and receiving hormone replacement therapy were of a higher socioeconomic status. They had a better-than-average diet and exercised more. It was actually the diet and exercise that were causing the lower incidence of heart disease, not the hormones themselves. There was a *correlation* between hormone replacement therapy and heart disease, but the hormones were *not causing* the decrease in heart disease.

System 1, however, doesn't want to do all that thinking! System 1 hears the correlation and automatically jumps to causative conclusions. If you want people to make these causal leaps, then you should make sure all the information makes a nice complete story, with no surprises. If you want people to think things through and instead engage System 2 thinking, then you need to jolt System 2 into action. We'll look at how to do that a little later in this chapter. For now, let's keep looking at how System 1 works.

 STRATEGIES

Strategy 90: When you want people to respond quickly, make a simple request that doesn't require them to think.

Use Coherent Stories

There's a whole chapter in this book on the power of stories. Not only does System 1 love a story, System 1 wants everything to hold together into a coherent whole.

If you want to activate System 1 and have people make a quick and intuitive decision, then you need to create a coherent story and stick with it. If you introduce an idea that's not part of the story, or if you change stories, then everything becomes disjointed and not coherent. System 1 will get uncomfortable, and turn to System 2 for assistance.

This is why simple, single messages are more effective than complex ones. Here's an example:

One company I work with creates animated videos. They've created the animated videos I use on my website and blog. You hear someone talking and while they're talking you see a hand drawing illustrations of whatever the message is. The company is called TruScribe, and animated videos are all they do. It's simple. It's easy for them to explain what they do. Their business is simple and they also explain it simply at their website (of course, with an animated video!).

Because it's easy to "get it," it's easy for people to take the next step and contact the company to talk about a possible engagement. If they also sold branding and logo services (which the owner used to do before he started TruScribe), it would be more complicated to understand who they are and what they do. Keeping it simple makes the story of their business coherent, which engages System 1.

STRATEGIES

Strategy 91: When you use a simple, coherent story, you make it more likely that people will make a decision or take an action.

The Power of Primes

If I show you the word

HOCKEY

And then I show you this word with a letter missing

P_CK

You will likely fill in the missing letter "U" to make

HOCKEY PUCK

But if I show you

SUITCASE

And then show you the same word

P_CK

You probably won't fill in the missing letter with a U. You'll fill it in with an A to make

PACK

How did you know whether to use U or A?

This is an example of something called "priming." System 1 is very susceptible to priming influences. Just by showing a word you can influence how someone will react to what follows. As we saw above, priming with the word HOCKEY made you see PUCK. Priming with the word SUITCASE made you see PACK.

Getting Mean with Monopoly

When my children were young we used to play the game Monopoly. It was one of my son's favorite games, and mine. It got to the point where no one would play with us anymore. We were too tough, too ruthless.

The games would go on forever because neither he nor I were willing to compromise or negotiate. "You're getting mean," my daughter would complain. And it was true. I could feel myself acting differently.

It turns out that my behavior was predictable. Kathleen Vohs, an associate professor of marketing at the University of Minnesota, researches the effect that money has on people. She doesn't even use actual money. Just the concept of money changes behavior.

In her research studies she gives people sentences to unscramble, some of which have money references, or she has them do tasks in a room where Monopoly money is on the table, or a picture of money is on a screen saver, or there is some other version of priming with money. Then she puts the participants into various situations. For example, someone walking through the room drops a box of pencils, or another (supposed) participant asks for help, or someone requests that the participant donate to a charity.

The findings are always the same. People who are primed with money ask for help less frequently, give help to others less often, donate less money, prefer to work or play alone, and put more physical space between themselves and others.

Vohs (Vohs 2006) concludes that the concept of money leads people to behave self-sufficiently. She defines self-sufficiency as a state where people work harder to attain personal goals and prefer to be separate from other people.

If you want people to be self-sufficient, prime them with the idea of, or pictures of, money. If you want people to be collaborative and help others, avoid the mention of, or pictures of, money.

 STRATEGIES

Strategy 92: When you want people to act independently, make a reference to money.

Strategy 93: When you want people to work with others or help others, *don't* refer to money.

Messages of Death

Sophie is preparing to give a speech at a benefit dinner. The benefit is for a nonprofit organization that funds medical teams to go to rural and impoverished parts of the world and perform operations for people who normally cannot afford medical treatment.

She's hoping that her speech will encourage the wealthy patrons at the benefit dinner to contribute even more money to the organization to support upcoming medical team visits.

If Sophie wants to be persuasive and get the donations, what should her message be? Specifically, should she mention death? Should she mention that without the medical teams and the operations more people will die? Will references to death cause the potential donors to give her more money or less money?

Before we answer that question, here's a related, but slightly different situation. Alyssa is also preparing to give a speech at a benefit dinner. Alyssa's benefit is for a local hospital. The hospital is trying to raise funds to build a new cancer wing. She's hoping that her speech will encourage the wealthy patrons at the dinner to donate money to support the new wing.

If Alyssa wants to be persuasive and get the donations, what should *her* message be? Should Alyssa mention death? Should she mention that without the new wing, more people in the community will die of cancer?

In the previous section we saw that money acts as a primer and can affect behavior. Just as you can prime with the concept of money, you can also prime with the concept of death or mortality.

In his book *Thinking, Fast and Slow,* Kahneman reviews the research on priming with death. In the research this is called either "mortality salience" or "terror management theory." Mentioning death could include statistics of how many people die of cancer, or you could talk about a particular person's death, or show a picture of someone dying. All of these things are considered "priming" with death.

When we hear a mention of death, it changes our behavior. When primed with messages of death, we engage in more "pro-social" behavior. This means that when primed with messages of death, we tend to behave in a way that's in keeping with the social norms of the groups we feel we belong too. Priming with death messages makes us follow the behavior of our tribe.

So should Sophie or Alyssa mention death in their speeches if they want to get more donations to their causes?

If giving money is part of the social norm of their tribe, then the answer would be yes. But it's not quite that simple. Someone who is wealthy and feels that wealthy people are expected to give back to their community *will* be more likely to donate money when they've been primed with death. However, they'll tend to donate only to causes that are part of their community.

Priming with messages of death makes us *less* empathetic. When we're primed with death, the activity in the part of the brain connected to empathy actually decreases. This is why people who are primed with messages of death are often less sensitive to people who are not like them.

Research shows that when people are primed with messages of death they become less sympathetic to people with disabilities and tend to blame victims rather than help them. Priming with messages of death also makes people more willing to obey authority.

All of this suggests that Alyssa should talk about death, since she is asking for money for the local community, but Sophie should avoid talking about death, since it will make people less empathetic toward "others."

 STRATEGIES

Strategy 94: When you want people to obey authority, use messages of death.

Strategy 95: When you want people to follow the social norms of the group they identify with, use messages of death.

Strategy 96: When you want people to be charitable to people within their community, use messages of death.

Strategy 97: When you want people to be sympathetic or charitable to people outside their community, avoid messages of death.

Anchoring: When a Number Is Not Just a Number

Look at the following multiplication problem. Don't actually do the multiplication, but estimate what you think the answer would be:

$$8 \times 7 \times 6 \times 5 \times 4 \times 3 \times 2 \times 1$$

When Amos Tversky and Daniel Kahneman (Kahneman 2011) asked people this question in their research, they found that the average estimate that people gave for the numbers as shown above was 2,250.

But when they showed the numbers in reverse order

$$1 \times 2 \times 3 \times 4 \times 5 \times 6 \times 7 \times 8$$

the average estimate was 512. (The correct answer, by the way, is 40,320.)

Starting with the larger number 8 resulted in a much higher estimate compared with starting with the smaller number 1.

Tversky and Kahneman called this tendency of one number to influence the estimate, perception, or preference of another number "anchoring and adjustment." People are susceptible to the starting reference point that you give. This starting reference point serves as an anchor and then changes what people expect from there.

For example, if a store advertises that customers can buy soda on sale, but that there's a limit of 10 bottles per customer, people will tend to buy more soda than if there's just a sale. Saying a limit of 10 sets 10 as the anchor point. When no number is mentioned then 0 becomes the anchor by default. With an anchor of 10 people end up buying more soda than if there's no anchor.

Put The Most Expensive Products and Services First

At my local carwash the prices are listed (all USD) as

Ultimate Exterior Supreme	$24.99
Exterior Supreme	$15.99
Ultimate Exterior	$11.99
Wheel Express	$ 8.99

The names could use some work, but the pricing makes use of anchoring. Since in English we read left to right, and top to bottom, the first price I read is $24.99. That sets the anchor. $15.99 and $11.99 don't sound so high in comparison to $24.99.

What if the choices were reversed?

Wheel Express	$ 8.99
Ultimate Exterior	$11.99
Exterior Supreme	$15.99
Ultimate Exterior Supreme	$24.99

Now the anchor is $8.99. $15.99 and $24.99 seem like a lot of money in comparison to $8.99.

$20 or $19.95?

If you look at the price of just about anything these days you'll see that the price is often specific: $29.95 instead of $30.00. Does it make a difference in anchoring whether you use a specific number or a more generic one? The answer is yes.

When you use a generic anchor, people adjust their estimate or price point more than with a specific anchor. So if the anchor is $29.75, people will tend to adjust to the more specific part of the number—in this case, raising or lowering by ten cents. They'll adjust to $29.85 or $29.65.

If the anchor is $30.00, they'll be more likely to adjust to the dollar part of the number, not the cents—for example, to $31 or $29.

This means that anchoring affects not just the number itself, but also which scale is used. The more specific initial price you use, the closer the final estimate will be to that initial price.

Arbitrary Anchoring

What's particularly odd about anchoring is that the anchor points don't even have to be related to the actual topic at hand.

In another study, Tversky and Kahneman (Kahneman 2011) had people spin a roulette wheel. The numbers on the wheel went from 1 to 100, but they rigged the wheel so it would always land on either the number 10 or the number 65. After spinning the wheel and getting a number, the researchers would then ask the participants to guess what percentage of countries in Africa were members of the United Nations.

Participants who spun the roulette wheel and landed on the number 10 guessed, on average, that 25 percent of the countries in Africa are in the United Nations. Participants who landed on the number 65 guessed, on average, that 45 percent of the countries in Africa are in the United Nations. Even a random number can act as an anchor.

A Quick Exercise in Arbitrary Anchoring

Here's an exercise for you:

1. If you're a US citizen, write down the last two digits of your Social Security number on a piece of paper. If you're not a US citizen, then just pick a two-digit number from 10 to 99 at random and write it down (don't read ahead before writing down your number!).

2. Now consider the following product offer:
   "You can purchase a trio of Lafite Rothschild wines: Château Paradis Casseuil from Bordeaux, Château d'Aussières from Languedoc, and Los Vascos from Chile."

3. Would you pay the number of dollars that is the last two digits of your Social Security number (or random number you wrote down) for this

trio of wines? For example, if the last two digits are 45 would you pay $45 for the three bottles of wine? Assuming you don't know what the wine is worth, answer the question without asking someone else about the price or looking it up online.

Dan Ariely conducted similar research (Ariely 2003). He showed students in a class several items, including wine, a cordless keyboard and mouse, a book on graphic design, and a box of Belgian chocolates. He passed out a sheet of paper that showed all the items in a list, and asked the students to write down the last two digits of their Social Security numbers. Next he asked them to turn those numbers into a dollar amount (that is, 45 became $45), and to mark next to each item whether they would pay that dollar amount for each of the products. Then he asked each student to write down the maximum amount they were willing to pay for each item. He used this number as a "bid" and the students with the highest number for each item paid that amount and bought the item.

Later he analyzed the data on the forms. The students with Social Security numbers ending in digits from 80 to 99 bid the highest amounts (an average of $56). Those with digits from 1 to 20 bid the lowest (an average of $16). When asked whether they thought that writing down the last two digits of their Social Security numbers had influenced their bids, the students said no, not at all.

 STRATEGIES

Strategy 98: When you want people to accept a high number, anchor with a high number.

Strategy 99: When you want people to accept a low number, anchor with a low number.

Strategy 100: To influence how people perceive prices and make numerical estimates, use an arbitrary number to act as an anchor.

Strategy 101: When you want people to choose a higher level of product or service, start your list with the highest level of service and the highest price.

Strategy 102: When you want people to stay close to your initial anchor price, use a very specific anchor.

Strategy 103: When you want people to consider prices that are different than your initial anchor price, use a less specific anchor.

Familiarity Breeds *Content*

Why are chain restaurants and stores so successful? One reason is because each chain restaurant or store looks the same and sells similar products—and in many cases, identical products—as every other store or restaurant in that chain.

Although there's a part of the brain that likes novelty, too much novelty, too often, makes us nervous. We like things to be familiar. When things are familiar, System 1 continues operating. System 1 equates familiar with good.

THE EXPOSURE EFFECT

The more we are exposed to something, the more familiar it is and the more we think it is "good." This is called the "exposure effect." This effect peaks at around five to seven exposures, at which point we start wanting novelty.

Familiarity Makes It True

Not only does System 1 connect familiarity with goodness, it also makes a leap to truth:

Familiar = Good + True

This is an interesting leap that our System 1 thinking makes. Just because something is familiar doesn't actually mean it's true. But if we see or hear about something a lot, our System 1 thinking equates the familiarity and goodness it feels with it also being true.

Remember, if you want to keep all of this in System 1 and not "awaken" System 2, then you should also keep your message coherent and simple:

Simple + Familiar = Good and True

Any reduction of cognitive strain will make the message seem truer.

When It's Familiar, We Think It's More Likely to Recur

In October 2012 New York City experienced a powerful hurricane (Hurricane Sandy). How likely is it that New York City will have a superstorm in the next five years?

If you had asked people that question before October 2012—before the storm—you would have gotten a different answer than if you asked them in November 2012—after the storm.

When something is familiar—when our memory of an experience is recent—we tend to overestimate the likelihood that the experience will happen again. When something is unfamiliar—when we don't have a recent memory of it—then we tend to underestimate the likelihood that the experience will happen again. Because of this familiarity effect, we have a hard time accurately estimating the probability that a specific event will occur.

You can use this familiarity effect to get people to do stuff. For example, if you want people to purchase flood insurance, the best time to ask them is right after a flood is in the news. People who have recently experienced a flood or heard about a flood will overestimate the likelihood that a flood will happen to them in the future.

STRATEGIES

Strategy 104: When you want people to think of a product or idea in a positive way, make that product or idea familiar to them.

Strategy 105: When you want people to think what you have is good and true, keep the message simple and expose them to it five to seven times.

Strategy 106: When you want people to think that a similar event is likely to happen again, ask them right after the first event occurs.

Strategy 107: When you want people to *underestimate* the likelihood of an event occurring again, ask them about a similar event that *hasn't* occurred recently.

Strategy 108: When you want people to *overestimate* the likelihood of an event occurring again, ask them about a similar event that *has* occurred recently.

Make It Hard to Read

Here's a word problem for you to solve:

> In a lake there is a patch of lily pads. Every day the patch doubles in size. If it takes 48 days for the patch to cover the entire lake, how long would it take for the patch to cover half of the lake?

> 24 days or 47 days?

Shane Frederick uses this problem on his Cognitive Reflection Test. In his experiments he showed the problem to half of the participants in a clear font similar to what you just read above. The other half of the participants saw the problem in type that was hard to read, like below:

In a lake there is a patch of lily pads. Every day the patch doubles in size. If it takes 48 days for the patch to cover the entire lake, how long would it take for the patch to cover half of the lake?

24 days or 47 days?

Did the readability of the font make a difference? Did people get the problem wrong or right with different fonts? (The right answer, by the way, is 47 days.)

Yes, the font did make a difference, but perhaps not in the way you might think. Ninety percent of the people in the study got the problem *wrong* when it was in the *larger, easy-to-read font.* Only 35 percent got the problem wrong when it was in the hard-to-read font.

When a font is easy to read, System 1 thinking does its usual thing—it makes quick decisions, which are not always accurate. When a font is harder to read, System 1 gives up and System 2 takes over. That means people will think harder and more analytically when a font is hard to read.

I'm *not* suggesting that writers and designers should intentionally make fonts hard to read all the time, but these findings do suggest that we pause and think about whether we're all inadvertently or purposely encouraging people not to think about what they're reading when the font is large and easy to read.

 STRATEGIES

Strategy 109: When you want people to respond quickly to what they're reading, make it easy to read.

Strategy 110: When you want people to use more thought or analysis before responding to what they read, make it more difficult to read.

Lulled with the Status Quo

In his book, *Thinking, Fast and Slow,* Daniel Kahneman poses this question:

"How many animals of each kind did Moses take into the ark?"

What did you answer? Two animals of each kind?

Well, actually, Moses didn't take any animals into the ark. That was Noah. As you read the sentence your System 1 thinking kicked in: "Oh, yeah, animals and the ark… it was two." Your System 1 thinking doesn't work very hard. As long as everything is going along as your brain expects, then System 1 does the minimal amount of thinking necessary, and therefore is prone to making these kinds of mistakes. Even though the sentence had Moses and not Noah in it, both are biblical references and therefore you didn't notice the discrepancy.

What if I ask you this question:

"How many animals of each kind did James Bond take into the ark?"

Even if you don't know who James Bond is, you won't be lulled into thinking this is a valid question. This is because James Bond is not the name that System 1 expects in this sentence. As soon as something happens that System 1 does not expect, it turns everything over to System 2.

System 2 sees right away that the question is invalid. System 1 is constantly looking for what is "normal." Kahneman says that the function of System 1 is to maintain and update a model of your personal world so you know at all times what is normal. When something is not "normal," then System 1 turns to System 2 for analysis and assistance.

System 2 does cow jumping. The previous sentence isn't right, is it? You noticed right away that there was a problem. Why did she write, "System 2 does cow jumping?" Your System 1 did the initial reading, but when it saw that sentence it stopped and asked System 2 for an assist.

If you want people to think about something rather than just glossing over the information, then you may need to surprise them in order to activate System 2 thinking.

When I give speeches or teach a workshop I include various surprises during my talk. I say something that people aren't expecting. I push a hidden button to make a loud air horn sound, or a show a picture that's not what people expect to see. By building in some surprise, I keep System 2 thinking awake during my sessions.

STRATEGIES

Strategy 111: When you want people to make quick decisions without thinking, don't do anything surprising.

Strategy 112: When you want people to think more carefully, do something unexpected.

Make People Uncomfortable

You're going to speak in front of your local city council to convince them to convert a particular street into a pedestrian mall. You have lots of data about why this is a good idea, and how doing this in other nearby towns has resulted in more business for the local merchants, and so on. But you also know that you have an uphill battle. Others have tried talking to the city council about this before and gotten nowhere. How can you get through?

It's likely that the city council members have a "confirmation bias." People tend to pay attention to what they already believe, and filter out information that doesn't fit with their opinions and beliefs.

If you present your data to the council about the benefits of pedestrian malls, they probably won't listen. They'll filter it out because it doesn't fit the conclusion they've already come to, which is that they don't like or want a pedestrian mall.

You can break through these biases, however. Here's what you need to do:

1. Start by bringing up, and agreeing with, what your audience already believes.

    For example, you might start with the council's concerns that a pedestrian mall will make it hard for people to find parking spots close to their favorite merchants. Instead of launching into the solution for this problem, start with exactly what they believe: "Pedestrian malls take away critical parking spots." "Yes!" your audience will be thinking, "That's right! Pedestrian malls make parking impossible." Now that you've agreed with them on this point, they'll be more likely to listen to you.

2. Introduce cognitive dissonance.

    Cognitive dissonance refers to the idea that people are uncomfortable holding views, opinions, or beliefs that contradict each other. In this example, your audience believes that pedestrian malls take away parking spots, that parking spots are important for business, and that if you take away parking you reduce business. Your audience doesn't think that these ideas conflict, so they don't have any cognitive dissonance.

    But next you present them with research from a reputable source showing that towns that implement pedestrian malls have a 30 percent increase in local business sales. Now the city council has cognitive dissonance. They want the increase in sales, but that doesn't agree with their opinion about the parking problems that they believe go hand in hand with pedestrian malls.

    Cognitive dissonance is uncomfortable. The city council is now uncomfortable. People will take action to get rid of cognitive dissonance.

3. Reduce the cognitive dissonance.

    You started by agreeing with the city council and then you introduced the research data that resulted in cognitive dissonance. Now you must immediately say something that rids them of their uncomfortable cognitive dissonance.

    For example, you could now make the point that a pedestrian mall is needed to relieve the current traffic and parking congestion. Shoppers in the current business area sometimes have to park three blocks away and then try to cross very busy intersections with a lot of traffic. Traffic congestion is an impediment to shoppers. So the pedestrian mall will actually solve the congestion problem and increase sales.

You need to provide a quick solution to ease the pain of their cognitive dissonance. They'll be so relieved that they'll be more likely to agree with your proposal.

STRATEGIES

Strategy 113: When trying to break through a confirmation bias, start by telling people something they already know and agree with.

Strategy 114: When trying to break through a confirmation bias, use cognitive dissonance to make people uncomfortable for a moment.

Strategy 115: Once you establish cognitive dissonance, provide an answer or solution that relieves people's discomfort. You'll be a hero for making them comfortable while also solving the problem, and you will therefore break through the confirmation bias.

Craving Certainty

We vary in terms of how much ambiguity we can handle without feeling uncomfortable. But everyone feels some amount of discomfort when things are ambiguous or uncertain.

There's a reason for this feeling of discomfort during uncertainty. When researchers look at activity in the brain during times of ambiguity or uncertainty they can see an increase in activity in the amygdala (Hsu 2005). The amygdala is where emotions are processed. Our reaction to uncertainty shows the same brain pattern as when we're physically threatened: increased activity in the amygdala.

Let's say you're thinking about upgrading your phone, and the salesperson at the phone store is offering you several different plans to choose from. You don't know what to do. You feel ambiguous and uncertain. This feeling is uncomfortable, and you'll likely behave in one of two ways:

1. To make the uncomfortable, ambiguous feeling go away, you might just decide not to decide, and walk out of the store.
2. If you have a "go-to guy," you will call him or her. People who research consumer purchases of electronics often talk about the importance of the go-to guy in the decision-making process. If you know someone who will know what to do, then you'll probably take his or her advice.

People who feel ambiguous or uncertain are suggestible. You can influence their decisions using one or all of these strategies:

- Take away the ambiguity (offer only one cell phone plan).
- Provide an expert who will help them decide (a go-to guy for them if they don't have one).
- Have an easy solution to the problem or decision ready to go.

You can even make it more likely that people will make a decision if you do the following:

1. Introduce ambiguity and uncertainty, just enough to make them uncomfortable.
2. Introduce a solution that will make the feeling of uncertainty go away.

 STRATEGIES

Strategy 116: To propel people to action, use ambiguity and uncertainty.

Strategy 117: To make ambiguity go away, provide an easy solution that resolves the ambiguity.

Don't Make People Think Too Much or Too Long

When I teach workshops I often ask people this question:

> Assuming that you're really interested in the topic, and that the presenter is a great presenter, how long do you think you can listen to the speaker without your mind starting to wander, without thinking of what you might have for dinner that night, or about an important message you forgot to respond to?

I usually get a range of answers. Some people say an hour, some say two hours, and some say three minutes. An hour or two is really generous! In fact, no matter how interested you are in the topic or how good the presenter is, it will be very hard for you to keep listening and stay engaged for that long, unless you're in a flow state (see Chapter 7, "The Desire For Mastery").

Certainly we can watch a movie for two hours and stay engaged (if it's a good movie), but watching a movie is not the same as System 2 effortful thinking. After only 20 minutes of hard thinking you've used up all the glucose in the brain that's needed for effortful thinking.

If you want people to learn, remember, and pay attention, then you need to think in terms of a maximum of 20-minute chunks. People will need a break every 20 minutes. This can be a stretch break where people literally stand up and move around, a snack break, a social break where they talk to others, a short nap, or anything else that gives them a break from System 2 effortful thinking.

If you don't give people a break, if you go beyond the 20-minute limit, then people won't be doing their best thinking or really paying attention.

STRATEGIES

Strategy 118: To get people to truly grasp what you're telling them, build in breaks at least every 20 minutes.

To Sound Profound, Make Sure Rhymes Abound

We're all familiar with proverbs, wise sayings such as

A bird in the hand is worth two in the bush.
A stitch in time saves nine.
A closed mouth catches no flies.

What you may not realize is that phrases that rhyme are believed to be more profound. So I can say,

Woes unite foes

Or

Woes unite enemies

Both phrases have the same meaning, but the first will be thought to be more profound because it rhymes.

STRATEGIES

Strategy 119: When you want to come across as smart or when you simply want to make a point, use a quote that rhymes.

Simple Names Are Best

My last name is Weinschenk. I'd probably sell more consulting, more training, and more books if my name were Walters, Wilson, or any other name that's easy to pronounce.

Research shows that people believe others are more credible if they have a name that is easy to pronounce. You may not be able to do anything about your name, but if you're naming a product or service, choose an easy-to-pronounce name if you want to appear more credible.

 STRATEGIES

Strategy 120: To establish credibility with your audience, choose a product or service name that's easy to pronounce.

How to Get People to Remember Stuff

You're on the phone talking to someone who's giving you a message. She's telling you that you need to call someone right away, and she's giving you the name and number you're supposed to call. But you don't have a pen or paper to write down the information.

It's very easy to forget the name and number in this situation. You resort to strategies to remember the information, such as repeating the name and number over and over. You try to get off the phone as quickly as possible so you can make the call right away while the phone number is still running through your head.

And yet you probably have many phone numbers memorized without even trying very hard. Why are some things harder to remember than others? How do you get people to remember stuff?

Trying to remember a phone number is an example of working memory. There's only so much you can hold in working memory before you forget it entirely. Information in working memory is easily interfered with.

Stress Reduces Memory

If you're trying to remember a name and phone number, and someone starts talking to you at the same time, you're probably going to get very annoyed. You're also going to forget the name and number. If you don't concentrate, you'll lose it from working memory. This is because working memory is tied to your ability to focus attention. In order to maintain information in your working memory, you must keep focusing your attention on it.

Scans of brain activity using functional magnetic resonance imaging (fMRI) show that there is less activity in the prefrontal cortex (the part of the brain right behind the forehead) when you're under stress; that is, stress reduces the effectiveness of working memory.

REDUCE SENSORY INPUT

Interestingly, there is an inverse relationship between working memory and the amount of sensory input you're processing at one time. People who have high-functioning working memories are better able to screen out what's going on around them. The prefrontal cortex is deciding what you should pay attention to. If you can stop paying attention to all the sensory stimuli around you, and instead focus your attention on just the one thing in your working memory, then you can remember it.

Use It Or Lose It

If you want people to move information from working memory into long-term memory, then you have to get them to either repeat it a lot or connect it to something they already know.

Let's say that you have a new step you want to introduce to your sales process. You gather your sales team in a room and tell them about the new step and ask if they've "got it." Everyone nods their head yes. You aren't sure, so you ask them to explain it back to you. They are able to do that so now you are convinced that they've learned the new step and will remember it.

They will, won't they?

Actually, one exposure to the information is probably not enough. You'll need more repetitions. Repetition physically changes your brain. There are 10 billion neurons in the brain that store information. Electrical impulses flow through a neuron and are moved by neuron-transmitting chemicals across the synaptic gap between neurons. Neurons in the brain fire every time we repeat a word, phrase, song, or phone number to ourselves. Memories are stored as patterns of connections between neurons. When two neurons are activated, the connections between them are strengthened.

If the information is repeated enough times, the neurons form a firing trace. Once the trace is formed, then just starting the sequence triggers the rest of the items, and the memory appears. This is why we need exposure to information over and over in order for it to stick.

Experience causes physical changes in the brain. In a few seconds new circuits are formed that can change forever the way we think about something or remember information.

In order for the firing trace to be formed, however, we need to repeat things several times. How many times depends on how complicated the information is, and how connected it is to something we already know.

If I ask you to add one simple step to a sales process you already know very well, then I may only need to repeat that information three times before a firing trace is established. But if the step of the sales process is complicated, or if you're not very familiar with the rest of the sales process, I'll probably need to repeat it five to seven times before the firing trace is strong enough for you to easily pull it out of memory.

Losing the Middle

You're at a conference listening to a presentation. When the presentation is finished, you meet your friend in the lobby of the hotel. "What was the talk about?" she asks. You're most likely to remember what was seen and heard at the end of the talk, but not so much about the beginning or middle of the talk.

This is called the Recency Effect: we tend to remember what happened most recently.

If, however, your phone vibrates during the presentation, and you step out for a minute to take a call and then go back in to the presentation, you are most likely to remember the beginning of the presentation and forget the ending.

This is called the Suffix Effect: if we're interrupted, then we tend to remember the beginning of the section that occurred before the interruption.

Whether the Recency Effect or Suffix Effect is operating, we tend to forget whatever is in the middle.

People Remember Concrete Words and Ideas More Than Abstract Ones

Let's say I'm preparing an argument about a right-to-work law (a hot topic in the US as I write this book). I could talk to you about the idea this way:

> The right-to-work law sharply limits labor rights. It bans workplace rules that make union membership a condition of employment for government workers. It denies workers freedom of choice.

Here's another way to talk about it:

The right-to-work law makes paying union dues voluntary. People can still belong to a union. It will be their choice. They can't force their coworkers to give their money to a private organization.

Putting politics aside, let's just look at the wording of these two paragraphs. The top paragraph refers to "labor rights," "workplace rules," "condition of employment," and "freedom of choice."

The second paragraph refers to "paying union dues," "force their coworkers," and "give money."

The first paragraph has more abstract concepts; the second has more concrete words and ideas.

If you were running for political office and wanted people to remember your position on right-to-work, you should give the message in concrete terms since people will remember words that are concrete more than words that are abstract.

 STRATEGIES

Strategy 121: When you want people to remember something, reduce the amount of sensory input and stress they experience.

Strategy 122: When you want people to remember something, repeat their exposure to it and have them actively repeat the information.

Strategy 123: When you want people to remember something, present that "something" at the beginning or end of an event, not in the middle.

Strategy 124: When you want people to remember what you have to say, use concrete words rather than abstract ones.

The Schematics in Your Head

If I ask you to describe what a "head" is, you might talk about the brain, hair, eyes, nose, ears, skin, neck, and so on. A head is made up of many things, but you've gathered all that information together and called it "head."

Similarly I could talk about the concept of an "eye." And you would think about all the things that make up an eye: the eyeball, iris, eyelash, eyelid, and so on. Psychologists call these groupings "schemas."

Just one schema helps organize a lot of information. You use schemas to store information in, and retrieve information out of, your long-term memory. You have schemas for more than just concrete things like "head" and "eye." You can have a schema for more abstract things, such as "the role that my job has in my life." Even more significant is the idea that you filter incoming information based on your schema.

EXPERTS HAVE MORE INFORMATION STORED AS A SCHEMA

The more expert someone is at something, the more organized and powerful her schema will be. For example, someone who's new to the game of chess needs a lot of little schemas:

- Schema 1: How to set up the pieces on the board
- Schema 2: How a queen can move
- And so on

But an expert chess player can pile a lot of information into one schema with ease. She can look at a chessboard in the middle of a game and tell you what some of the starting moves were, the strategies for each player, and what the next move is likely to be. She could certainly recite how to set up the board and how each piece can move.

What would take many schemas for the novice player, the expert player has stored in one schema. This makes retrieval of information faster and easier, and makes it easier for the expert to put new information about chess into long-term memory. The expert can remember a lot of information as one single chunk.

Does My Schema Match Yours?

People have schemas for all kinds of things, and they use these schemas to filter and respond to information.

In his book *What Makes Your Brain Happy and Why You Should Do the Opposite* (DiSalvo 2011), David DiSalvo gives the example of someone interviewing for a job. If you're the interviewer, you have a particular schema in your head about what the job is, what working at your organization is like, the last person who did the job, and so on. This schema affects how you describe the job to people who interview for it, and you also use the schema to judge whether a candidate is a good fit.

On the other side, people who come for an interview have a schema about what their ideal job would be. They even have a schema about your company. Their schemas influence how they act, what they say, and whether they accept a job offer.

You can see how it would be easy for schemas to clash. A candidate might be looking for a job that isn't too demanding, so she can fit it into the responsibilities of caring for children and her parents who are aging. Using her schema, she might decide that your job is not a good fit. On the other hand, you might have a schema about the job as a demanding one. You might think that the job is tough and will take a lot of time, dedication, and late nights, but that these are good things since the person who has the job will learn a lot and be able to advance. Your schema could be very different than your candidate's schema for the same job opening.

When schemas are unconscious and don't match, misunderstandings occur.

If you want people to do stuff, like accept a job offer, you need to understand what schema or schemas are operating for them around the topic, so you can adjust how you interact with them and what information you provide.

Most of us think that we know what other people's schemas are, but often we're just projecting our schema onto others.

This was brought home to me several years ago. I worked for a consulting company and reported to the president of the company. He sent me to a weeklong leadership training session. The company teaching the training session also conducted a "360 review." This meant that my boss, my boss's boss, my peers, and the people who worked for me all completed long questionnaires about me, my work, my communication skills, and so on. I filled out some of the questionnaires too.

At the training session we received reports with summaries from the questionnaires. One of the summaries compared

- Which skills I thought were most important for my job
- Which skills I thought my boss would think were the most important for my job
- Which skills my boss said were most important to him

There were 12 different skills and we had to rank them from 1 to 12, with 1 being most important and 12 being least important.

I got along well with my boss, communicated with him often, spoke several times a year about goals, and felt that we understood each other well. You can imagine, then, my surprise to find out that I had been using the wrong schema. The skills he rated as the most important were at the bottom of my list and vice versa.

Some of the strategies in this book work even if you don't know the people you're trying to get to do stuff. For example, most people react to messages of scarcity or death in similar ways. But many of the strategies in the book require you to understand the schema at work for a particular individual if you're going to use the strategy effectively.

STRATEGIES

Strategy 125: To get people to do stuff, get to know them and their sche-mas so you can tailor your strategy to fit how they look at the world.

Strategy 126: Closely examine your assumptions about schemas—we tend to think our schemas are the same as those of the people we're interacting with, but our schemas might be different.

Two Words That Can Change Everything

Could something as simple as having people ask themselves a question that starts with "Will I" change behavior? The answer is yes!

Ibrahim Senay (Senay 2010) tested the effect on behavior of people using "I will" versus "Will I." For example, "I will exercise three times a week," versus "Will I exercise three times a week?" It seems like common sense that if people make a statement ("I will") that would be more powerful than if they ask a question ("Will I").

But research shows otherwise. When people phrased the intention as a question, they were more likely to actually carry out the behavior. Senay's theory is that when people ask themselves a question it inspires them to be intrinsically motivated, and that makes them more likely to follow through.

STRATEGIES

Strategy 127: When you can get people to ask themselves a question beginning with "Will I …," you're more likely to get them to act on the statement.

Metaphors Have the Power to Change How We Think

The statement "Crime is plaguing our cities" is a metaphor. Crime is not really a plague. But it can be *like* a plague. Here are some other common metaphors:

He has the heart of a lion.
She jumped for joy.
He's rolling in dough.
It's raining cats and dogs.
I'm heartbroken.

Metaphors aren't just an expressive way to communicate a thought. Metaphors are a frame and as such, they affect behavior.

Paul Thibodeau (Thibodeau 2011) asked people to work in groups to come up with solutions to social problems. He gave people descriptions of the crime problem in various cities, as well as statistics on crime in the cities. Then he asked them to come up with solutions to the crime problems.

Some of the people were given descriptions that used wild animal metaphors, for example, crime is a "wild beast preying on the city" or "lurking in neighborhoods." Others were given descriptions that used disease metaphors, for example, crime is a "virus infecting the city" or "plaguing neighborhoods."

How did the metaphors affect the solutions?

When people were given the wild animal metaphors, 75 percent of their solutions revolved around police and law enforcement. Only 25 percent of the solutions mentioned social programs, such as jobs, housing, or education. When the medical metaphors were used, then the solutions were 56 percent law enforcement and 44 percent social programs.

Interestingly, when the participants were asked whether the description influenced their solution, most said no. They believed that the statistical data on crime was the major or only influence. They were not aware that their solution might have been influenced by a metaphor.

Metaphors have a deep influence on how people think about a topic, and on the solutions and decisions they come up with. Think carefully about how you describe a situation and what metaphors you're using. The metaphors you use will change others' perceptions about the issue and the likely solutions.

STRATEGIES

Strategy 128: Carefully choose the metaphors you use to describe a situation to others. The metaphor frames the question and affects the solution and outcome.

Seize the Moment

I was listening to one of my favorite podcasts while jogging outside. Before the particular podcast started, the podcast producer made a pitch for donations to the podcast. He asked listeners to text a few simple characters to a text number. If I did that, a $10 donation would be made to the podcast. I slowed to a walk for the 10 seconds it took me to send the text.

If he had asked me to go online to the website and donate money, that wouldn't have been as specific—and it wouldn't have involved an impulse action. I wouldn't have stopped my exercise in order to go to a website and navigate through the steps to donate right then. And chances are high that by the time I got back home after exercising I would forget what to do, or even that I had wanted to donate.

I had been listening to this podcast for years. Why hadn't I donated before? Did I not realize that I wasn't paying for the podcasts? No, I knew I wasn't buying them. I was "subscribed" and was downloading them for free. Am I very poor and can't afford to give money? Or a cheapskate and just don't like donating? No, none of those are true.

Do I not really like the podcast? No, I find great value and entertainment in it.

So why hadn't I donated yet? Because no one had ever told me exactly what to do and caught my impulse moment while I was listening to the podcast. No one had given me a specific action to take that I was able to take impulsively in the moment.

 STRATEGIES

Strategy 129: To get people to take an action, use their tendency to act on impulse.

Strategy 130: To encourage impulsive action, make your request specific, simple, and quick.

Time Is Money

If giving or donating money is what you want people to do, research shows that people are more likely to give money, and more likely to give *more* money, if you ask them to donate time first.

In *The Dragonfly Effect* (Aaker 2010), Jennifer Aaker describes a research study she did with Wendy Liu. They asked people to help fight lung cancer through the American Lung Cancer Foundation. People were first told about the mission of the American Lung Cancer Foundation, and then were told that the foundation was having a fundraising event. Half of the people were asked, "How much time would you like to donate to the American Lung Cancer Foundation?" The other half of the people were not asked that question.

When both groups were asked, "How much money would you donate to the American Lung Cancer Foundation?" the people who had not first been asked to donate time averaged pledges of $24.46. But the people who had first been asked to donate time averaged pledges of $36.44. The authors report that the same thing happened when people actually gave/donated money and weren't just asked for pledges.

It's hard to know exactly why this is. It could be the idea of concession (see Chapter 2, "The Need to Belong"), or perhaps some kind of priming by mentioning the word *donate* early on. But it's also possible that it has to do with the idea of invoking time.

STRATEGIES

Strategy 131: When you want people to spend more money, first ask them to spend more of their time.

People Value Experience More Than They Value Things

Perhaps the reason that invoking time results in people spending more money is that in mentioning time, you emphasize an *experience* with the product, rather than just the purchase.

What makes you happier? Having an experience or having a possession? Are you happier going on a trip with your family or are you happier buying a new TV and watching the Travel Channel with your family?

Ryan Howell (Howell 2012) asked people which they valued more: recent experiences they had versus recent things they had purchased. People reported that they were usually happier with the experiences. They also said that other people in their lives were made happier by the experiences than by the possessions.

Leaf Van Boven (Van Boven 2010) studied people over the span of several years and found that most people were made happier by spending money on experiences rather than on possessions.

One reason why time might be more important than money and that people value experiences more than possessions is that many experiences involve doing things with other people. It's that connectedness and social interaction that's important.

The idea of time being more important than money isn't true for all people, or for all purchases. Research shows that only a few people value things more than they value experiences. People who are emotionally insecure, wealthy, and considering a "luxury" purchase (for example, an expensive car) value the "thing" they are buying more than an experience.

If you're selling something or asking for a donation for a thing, see if you can turn that purchase or donation into an experience. For example, instead of selling concert tickets to people, sell the experience of people sharing music with their friends.

If you want to get people to donate to a charity, you'll get more and larger donations if you provide an experience rather than just ask for money. For example, sponsor a "walk and run" for your charity, or a benefit concert, or a dance. These experiences will result in more donations than giving an incentive that is a thing, such as a mug, an umbrella, a book, or a CD.

 STRATEGIES

Strategy 132: Sell people on the experience. They'll spend more money on an experience than they will on an item.

Wandering Minds

You're driving to work, thinking about work, and home, and your weekend plans, and before you know it, you've pulled into the parking lot of your office. You're surprised to realize that you don't even remember the drive. The last thing you really remember is getting into your car. What happened during the 20 minutes you were driving? You were "mind wandering."

How common is mind wandering? If you ask people that question, they estimate that mind wandering happens 10 percent of the time. But it's actually much more common.

According to Jonathan Schooler of UC Santa Barbara (Christoff 2009), your mind wanders at least 30 percent of the time when you're doing your normal day-to-day tasks, and in some cases—for example, when driving on an uncrowded highway—it might be as high as 70 percent.

Mind wandering is similar to, but not the same as, daydreaming. Psychologists use "daydreaming" to refer to any stray thoughts, fantasies, or stories you imagine, for example, winning the lottery, or being a famous celebrity. The term "mind wandering" is more specific, and refers to when you're doing one task and then you fade into thinking about something that's not related to that task.

Malia Mason (Mason 2007) recorded people's brain activity and correlated that to self-reports of mind wandering. When people reported that their mind was wandering their brains showed activity in several cortical regions that are also active when our brains are at rest. These areas are always operating in the background. So mind wandering is a natural part of how our brains work.

The Multitasking Mind Wanderer

Mind wandering allows one part of the brain to focus on the task at hand, and another part of the brain to keep a higher goal in mind. For example, while you're driving, you're paying attention to the road, but you're also thinking about the meeting you have when you get to your destination.

Mind wandering might be the closest thing we have to multitasking. Multitasking doesn't really exist. Research on multitasking shows that we don't really do more than one task at a time. What we really do is switch tasks quickly. Psychologists call it "task switching" instead of multitasking. (Meyer 1997). But mind wandering does allow us to switch focus from one idea to another, and then back again quickly. For example, you're reading an article about a medication that your doctor thinks you should take, but your mind wanders to the idea that you should make an appointment for a haircut.

The Creative Mind Wanderer

The researchers at UC Santa Barbara have shown that people whose minds wander a lot are more creative and better problem solvers. They're able to work on the task at hand, while simultaneously processing other information and making connections among ideas. Specifically, the ability to come in and out of mind wandering at will is very significant, and it's the hallmark of the most creative people.

Embracing the Wandering Mind

Now that you know that minds wander at least a third of the time, what can you or should you do about it?

- Build in breaks. We talked before about making sure that people have breaks. You might as well build them in, since people are taking them on their own through mind wandering even if you aren't.
- Don't be shy about grabbing attention. It's easy to distract people. Even if people are engrossed in a task, it will be easy to distract them.
- Assume distraction. The flip side of it being easy to grab attention is that it's easy to lose people. You'll need to be continually pulling them

back. For example, if you're speaking at a meeting, you need to change it up in order to bring people back. Moving to a different spot in the room or asking a question will help bring people back from their mind wandering.

- Let people mind wander. Mind wandering is not all bad. Since we know that mind wandering is related to creativity, try to change your attitude about it. If someone is sitting at her desk staring into space, she might be thinking about her dog, but she might also be doing creative thinking.

 STRATEGIES

Strategy 133: Accept the fact that people's minds are wandering at least a third of the time and use the strategies in this book to get their attention.

Get People to Stop Thinking

You've been working on a problem or idea that you can't seem to solve. Maybe you've been trying to figure out how to staff a project at work, and you just don't see how you can free up the right people to do the project. You don't have the answer yet, but it's lunchtime, and you're meeting a friend and need to run some errands too. On your way back from errands and lunch you're walking down the street and suddenly you get a flash of insight about how to staff the project.

These flashes of insight are quite common. In fact, this is how our brains solve problems. Friedrich August Kekulé is the scientist who discovered the ring structure of the chemical benzene. He told a story that he had a daydream of a snake seizing its own tail, and that's how he came up with the idea that the molecular structure of benzene is a ring.

These flashes of insight involve the basal ganglia of the brain. This is where dopamine is stored, and it's a part of the brain that operates outside of your conscious awareness.

When you're consciously trying to solve a problem, the prefrontal cortex is at work. If a problem requires "out-of-the-box" thinking, however, then you need to remove the problem temporarily from conscious awareness. If the conscious brain stops working on the problem, then the unconscious part of the brain can work on it instead. By doing a different, unrelated activity—taking a shower, going for a walk, mind wandering, or sleeping—you're able to connect information in new ways via your unconscious mental processing.

People can work consciously on problems for days, months, or even years and not solve them. If you want people to be great problem solvers and have these flashes of insight, then you need to have them

- Initially spend some time consciously working on the problem. Although flashes of insight come when people are *not* consciously working on a problem, the prefrontal cortex has to be able to first consciously set out what the problem is. So up-front conscious thought is critical.
- Stop working on the problem and do an unrelated activity. This is when the basal ganglia take over from the prefrontal cortex. Physical behavior that involves habit and automaticity is the best here. You want to let the prefrontal cortex go into rest mode. Flashes of insight come when the person is not only not thinking about the problem, but also is not thinking about *any* problem. This means that flashes of insight are most likely to occur when someone is walking, taking a shower, or doing an activity that doesn't require much thought and allows mind wandering.

 STRATEGIES

Strategy 134: When you want people to solve problems, especially creatively, let them stop thinking.

Strategy 135: To maximize problem-solving skills, build in nonstructured mind wandering time.

Shoulda, Woulda, Coulda: The Power of Regret

Of all the situations and feelings that motivate people to take action or motivate them to avoid a certain action, regret is one of the most powerful. We don't like to feel regret and we'll do a lot to avoid it. But you might be surprised to find out what makes us feel regret and how we get rid of it.

More opportunity equals more regret

The more choice and opportunity we have, the more regret we feel. The more we feel that we could have done something differently, the more regret we feel. If we feel that we had no choice in our decision or action, then we feel less regret.

Related to this idea of opportunity is the idea that the stronger and clearer a corrective action is, the more dissatisfied and disappointed people will feel.

For example, let's say you're choosing a restaurant for an upcoming special event. You have three great restaurants that are available on the date you want. You choose one of the three and negotiate the menu with the restaurant staff. At the last minute the restaurant calls and changes the menu you had planned. You resist initially, but eventually give up. You're not at all happy with the food they provide during the event.

You could have taken corrective action (insisted they stick with the menu) or picked a different restaurant to start with, or switched to one of the other restaurants. But you didn't do any of those things. So you had opportunity and you had clear corrective actions. In this situation you'll feel a lot of regret, dissatisfaction, and disappointment.

Contrast this with the following scenario: There's only one restaurant available on the date you want to hold the event. And it only offers one set of menu choices. There is no negotiation. Even though you might rate the food as good or as bad as in the first example, you'll feel less regret, less disappointment, and less dissatisfaction.

Regret Inspires Action

Because we don't like feeling regret, and because we feel the most regret about things we can fix, regret is actually a motivator for action. If we're feeling regret, then that's when we're highly likely to take action. And we'll often take an action to avoid regret before it happens.

THE OLDER YOU GET, THE LESS REGRET YOU FEEL

It may seem counterintuitive, but the older people get, the less regret they feel. This is because the older people get the less opportunity they have to change or fix things. They don't have forever to do things differently. Since regret is related to feeling that you have opportunities, people feel less regret the older they get.

 STRATEGIES

Strategy 136: When you want people to feel less regretful, offer them fewer choices.

Strategy 137: When you want people to take action, engage them while they're feeling regret.

Doing the Heavy Lifting

Do you think you'd make different decisions if you were holding something heavy in your hands than if you weren't? Sounds unlikely, but it's true.

Joshua Ackerman and John Bargh (Ackerman 2010) conducted research where they had candidates for job interviews hand in their resumes one of three ways. One candidate handed in her resume on regular printer paper. Another candidate handed in her resume on regular printer paper, but had it clipped to a light clipboard. A third candidate handed in her resume on regular printer paper, but had it clipped to a heavy clipboard. Then they had interviewers rate which candidates were the best for the job. The interviewers gave higher ratings to candidates whose resumes they were reading while holding a heavy clipboard.

Holding a heavy object while looking at a resume makes a job candidate appear more important. In fact, any idea you're considering while holding something heavy (for instance, a book) you will deem to be more important. The metaphor of an idea being "weighty" has a physical corollary.

The term for this is "embodied cognition," and it refers not only to how we translate the idea of weight, but also to several judgments that are all related to touch. The official term in psychology research is "haptic sensations." We are very influenced by the meaning that our sense of touch perceives.

You may be surprised to find out all the ways that these haptic sensations affect our perceptions and judgments. Besides the effect of a heavy object, people also react to these other haptic sensations:

- When people touch a rough object during a social interaction, for instance, if they're sitting on a chair with coarse wool upholstery, they rate the interaction more difficult than if they touch a soft object.
- When people touch a hard object, they rate a negotiation as more rigid than if they touch a soft object.
- When people hold a warm cup (for example, a warm cup of coffee), they judge the person they're interacting with to have a warmer personality than if they're holding a cup of cold liquid.

You can use these haptic sensations to get people to do stuff. If you want people to have easier interactions with others, then you might want to have soft furniture, not hard chairs, in your conference room, and use a soft fabric covering for them rather than a scratchy tweed. If you have an important client coming to your office, and you want her to feel warmly about you, get her a cup of hot coffee or tea in a mug that will transmit the heat before you start.

STRATEGIES

Strategy 138: When you want people to interact smoothly and flexibly, use soft objects and smooth fabrics.

Strategy 139: When you want people to perceive that what you're saying is important, have them hold something heavy.

Strategy 140: When you want people to react to you warmly, don't let them hold cold drinks. Give them a cup of something hot.

Case Studies:
Using Drivers
and Strategies in
the Real World

IF YOU'VE REACHED THIS POINT in the book, you should have a good handle on the seven motivational drivers, and the strategies for using each. In this chapter we'll look at how to put the drivers into action. To use them to get people to do stuff you have to

- Decide which driver or drivers best fit your situation.
- Decide which strategies to use for that driver.

In this chapter we'll walk through examples and case studies that will give you some experience with making these two decisions.

While I was writing this book, I asked my readers for their ideas of examples to use. I asked them to tell me what they want to get people to do. I've included many of their responses as case study examples, and added some of my own.

Before we start, though, there are a few principles to keep in mind:

You can combine drivers. It's possible that two or even three drivers will work for a particular situation, for example, the Need to Belong *and* Habits. It's OK to use more than one. When you pick your drivers it's also likely that there is more than one strategy within a driver that will work, for example, social validation *and* talking first to establish yourself as the leader for the Need to Belong driver.

Pick the drivers with the most power potential. Some drivers are more powerful than others. When there are several drivers that would be motivating for your particular situation, make sure you're making use of the most powerful driver. Here's the list of drivers from most powerful to least:

1. Instincts
2. The Power of Stories
3. Tricks of the Mind
4. The Need to Belong
5. The Desire for Mastery
6. Habits
7. Carrots and Sticks

When a particular situation could be addressed with the Power of Stories as well as by Carrots and Sticks, make sure to implement the Power of Stories solution. Then, when you have time and energy, you can add the Carrots and Sticks solution to it.

Customize as much as possible to the individual(s). The more you know about the person or people you're trying to get to do stuff, the more effective you'll be at picking a good motivator. For example, for your particular situation either Tricks of the Mind or the Need to Belong might work in general, but for the particular person the Need to Belong might be the most motivating.

Know which drivers are best for long-term change and for a short-term, automatic reaction. Some drivers are best for long-term change, and others for getting an automatic, quick reaction in the short term.

> Best for long-term change:
>> The Power of Stories
>> The Desire for Mastery
>> The Need to Belong
>> Habits

> Best for an automatic, quick reaction:
>> Instincts
>> Carrots and Sticks
>> Tricks of the Mind

Get people to want to do stuff. You may have realized as you've been reading the book that the easiest way to get people to do stuff is to get them to *want* to do stuff. The more you understand psychology, the better you'll be able to sync what you want people to do with what they want to do. Ultimately it's not about manipulation—it's about understanding.

Let's start using these ideas to make decisions about drivers and strategies for particular situations.

Get People to Donate Money

"I run the local branch of a nonprofit charity and I want people to donate money."

The best drivers to use are the Need to Belong and the Power of Stories.

The Power of Stories

Use the idea of a consistent self-persona. Connect the donation to the stories people tell around who they are, for example, "Since you're a person who cares about people in need…"

Have them take a small action first. Before asking them to donate money, encourage them to share information you provide on humanitarian relief with a friend, or see if they will volunteer next Saturday for two hours to organize relief supplies. This is especially important when they don't have an existing self-persona that would compel them to donate money to your cause. After they take the small action, they will have changed their self-persona and will be more likely to donate, since donating now fits with their self-persona.

Have them make a public commitment. Ask them to donate in a way that is public. For example, list them as a donor or have them share that they've donated online.

The Need to Belong

Use social validation. Show how many others have already donated. For example, at the Global Giving website, you'll see "Since 2002, 306,481 donors like you have given $76,920,248 to 7,120 projects. Wonderful!"

Use brain syncing. Talk to them one-on-one, make a presentation, or use video (with audio) so you can have the listener's brain sync with whoever is asking for the donation.

Convey your passion. Remember that emotions are contagious. Convey your passion for the project with your tone of voice to get others excited.

Use reciprocity. Give them something before you ask for the donation. For example, host a reception with free food, send free pens in the mail, give access to special information, or give any other small gift that sets up a feeling of indebtedness.

Use nouns rather than verbs. When you talk to people say "Will you be a donor?" rather than "Will you donate?" Using a noun stimulates the sense of belonging to a group of people who will donate and makes it more likely that they will in fact donate.

Get People to Take Initiative

"Jim is one of my employees. He is basically good at his job, but I want him to take more initiative. Instead of waiting for me to tell him what to do all the time, I want him to step up, decide what needs to be done, and do it."

The best drivers in this situation are the Desire for Mastery, Carrots and Sticks, and the Power of Stories.

The Power of Stories

Use story prompting. Jim may not think of himself as an initiator. He may not have a self-story as someone who starts projects on his own. If he doesn't, you can prompt the creation of a new story. Start labeling him as someone who does. Look for ways and situations to prompt him to think of himself as an initiator ("Last month when you initiated the project to...") or let him hear you tell others that he is an initiator, for example, copy him on an e-mail where you say to someone else, "Do you remember when Jim initiated the program to…."

Have Jim listen to other people's stories. Tell Jim stories about other people who are initiators. Better yet, have others share their own stories with Jim: "Andrew, would you take a few minutes sometime this week and tell Jim about how you put together and implemented your ideas on shortening the time-to-market cycle?"

The Desire for Mastery

Suggest autonomy. Let Jim know that he has control over what he does and how he does it.

Give opportunities to learn from mistakes. Taking initiative is often fraught with errors. Make sure that Jim knows that it's OK for him to make mistakes, but that you expect him to learn from them. His desire to master being an initiator will increase when he's allowed to make mistakes.

Give feedback. When you give Jim feedback when he makes mistakes, then his desire for mastery and to be an initiator will increase. Don't praise or punish him with the feedback. Make the feedback as objective as possible.

Get Someone to Hire You as an Employee

"I've applied for a job, and it's my dream job. I like the company and the position. I really want this job! Melanie is the person responsible for making the decision to choose me rather than all the other candidates. How can I get Melanie to offer me the job?"

The best drivers in this situation are Tricks of the Mind, Instincts, and the Need to Belong.

Tricks of the Mind

Activate System 1 thinking. You want Melanie to use System 1 (that is, easy and intuitive) thinking as much as possible. Actually, Melanie *is* using System 1 thinking. Your job is to get her to stay in System 1 thinking as much as possible. Make sure that when you talk about your background and experience that you have a coherent story that hangs together.

Make printed documents easy to read. Because you want to keep System 1 operating, make sure any printed material you give Melanie, such as a writing sample or a resume, is in a simple, legible font, in a large enough type size so it's easy to read. Don't use a background color that makes the text hard to read.

Don't do anything surprising. You might think that you need to do something different to make yourself stand out from the crowd, but when you're at the point of talking one-on-one to Melanie, you've already made it through an initial cut. You don't want to do anything at this point that's too surprising, since that would cause Melanie to switch from System 1 to System 2 thinking.

Make use of the confirmation bias. Because the confirmation bias exists, Melanie will be looking for information that fits with her existing beliefs. Ask enough questions so that you know what her schema is about the job. Then talk about things that she already knows and agrees with: "I know you want to hire people who will get along well with the rest of the team." Or, "In a recession like the one we are in, it's important to hire people who can hit the ground running."

Be the easy solution that makes ambiguity go away. People don't like ambiguity. Not knowing whom to hire creates ambiguity and therefore an uncomfortable feeling. Make hiring you the easy solution. Avoid causing any complications (for example, saying that you can't start the job for two months because you're committed to a Caribbean sailing excursion with your friends).

Make your name easy to say. Remember that when your name is long or hard to pronounce, it erodes your credibility and makes what should seem easy (hiring you) now seem hard. You might not be able to change your name just to get hired, but see if you can provide an easy version: "My name is Aloysius, but most people call me Al." For my name I give people a phonetic spelling, writing "Wine-shank" on a piece of paper and giving them the piece of paper, so that it is easier for them to pronounce.

Focus on and prepare for the beginning and end of your interview. Remember that people tend to forget the middle of a conversation, so make sure you open the conversation with important points and that you end with important points.

Instincts

Use scarcity and fear of losing. If only 5 percent of graphic designers have a master's degree, and if you're one of that 5 percent, make sure to mention that. Someone who has earned a master's degree is scarce, and therefore more valuable. If you have another offer, make sure you mention that so that Melanie will know you're in demand. And if you're supposed to let the other company know by a certain date, make sure to mention that as well. The idea that Melanie might lose you to a competitor will make her more likely to act fast.

The Need to Belong

Joining a new company or organization as an employee is like joining a tribe. A lot of our social interactions and identification take place through our work. Many of the strategies that have to do with the need to belong are active when you want someone to hire you.

Try as much as possible for an in-person interview. You want to be able to use many of the ideas in the Need to Belong chapter, and that means that you want to meet face-to-face. You won't be able to use many of the strategies on the phone. The least effective is to do everything via mail or email. You need to be able to talk directly to Melanie. You want to at least speak to Melanie remotely so you can use brain syncing between the speaker and listener.

Use bonding. Since you want to establish rapport with Melanie, try to do something together, synchronously, in order to bond. For example, see if the two of you can laugh at the same time about something. Do this early on in the meeting.

Be a leader. You'll be more persuasive with Melanie if you're seen as a leader. Talk first when you meet, but make it short—talking first (good thing) is not the same as dominating the entire conversation (bad thing).

Watch your language. Speak confidently. Don't speak too fast or too slow. Communicate with passion, energy, and enthusiasm.

Be mindful of your body language. Make sure to sit and stand up straight. Don't lean on furniture. Don't sit too far forward (conveys too much eagerness) or too far back (conveys disinterest). Practice some of your conversation in front of a mirror and make sure your hand gestures match your message. Remember to look Melanie straight in the eyes sometimes and to smile slightly while talking.

Use similarity and attractiveness. Dress similarly to the way Melanie and others at her level and one level below her are dressed. You want Melanie to believe that you'll fit in. Find out what people at the job level you are applying to would dress like and do a really nice version of that. For example, if Melanie wears business casual and her staff dresses casually in jeans, try for something in between. If Melanie is wearing a business suit and her staff are all in jeans and T-shirts, you should wear business casual. If Melanie and her staff are all wearing suits, you should wear a suit. The idea is to build rapport by showing you are one of the tribe. If you've been working with someone in recruiting or Human Resources, you can ask them what the proper attire is for the office. They like it when candidates ask. In addition, do your best to be as attractive as possible. Make sure you have a great haircut, good skin-care, pressed clothes, shoes in good condition, and so on. You may not have celebrity good looks, but you can take steps to be as attractive as possible.

Imitate body movements and gestures. See if you can imitate a few of Melanie's body gestures and movements. If Melanie crosses one leg over another you can do the same. If she places her hands palms down on the table you can do the same. Don't make it too obvious, but if you can imitate a few of her movements it will help build rapport.

Drop names. Although indiscriminate and excessive name dropping can be annoying, it will help you a lot to mention companies you've worked for that Melanie may recognize. If you've worked with or for specific people that she knows, you definitely want to mention that: "When I was an analyst at Disney I worked with someone I believe you know, John Milton." That establishes you as being in a similar tribe.

Even better than name dropping: use social validation. Get a reference or referral from someone Melanie knows personally. Have him or her call or write to Melanie, preferably *before* your interview. This shows that others have already brought you into the tribe, and therefore, Melanie will be more likely to do the same.

Get Someone to Accept a Job Offer

"I've been interviewing candidates for an open position in my department. I've picked Lisa as the best candidate and I'm going to offer her the job. I really want her to take it so I can end the hiring process, get on with my other work, and be certain that I have a great addition to the team. What can I do to get Lisa to take the job?"

The best drivers to use in this situation are Instincts, the Power of Stories, the Need to Belong, and the Desire for Mastery.

The Power of Stories

Tie into Lisa's self-persona stories. As Lisa goes through the interview process you might be able to figure out what self-stories she has about her work. Tap into these stories to make your job and organization a better fit with her stories:

- "I know that it's important to you that you feel that you're making a difference. This job is one where you can really feel that…"
- "I know that you're someone who values work/life balance. This job will help you achieve that…"
- "Based on our conversations during the interview process, I've gathered that you are an ambitious person. This job will give you opportunities to…"

The Desire for Mastery

Stress new learning. Lisa will like the idea that there's an opportunity to learn new skills on the job. Stress all the new things she will learn.

Imply an elite corps. We like to feel that we're special and part of a small group who can do a task. If you tell Lisa, "The work for this job requires a very special skill set and experience. There aren't very many people who have the right requirements. We were so happy to find you since you're one of those few," then she'll be more likely to accept the job.

Mention autonomy. We like to feel that we have autonomy in our work. If you tell Lisa, "You'll have the opportunity in this job to do the work in the way you think best. You'll have a lot of control over how you work," then she'll be more likely to take the job.

Point out the challenge of the job. We like to feel that we're up for a challenge. If you say to Lisa, "This isn't an easy job. To do it well is not impossible, but it's challenging. We believe you have the skills and knowledge to succeed," then she'll be more interested in the job.

Don't make it too easy. If Lisa feels that she had to work to get the job, she'll want it even more. Make sure that there's a process for getting the job that requires some hurdles to be overcome. Ask her to interview with more than one person and ask her to submit a resume and a portfolio. Ask for references and check them. Taking these steps will make it more likely that Lisa will accept the job.

Instincts

Activate the idea of scarcity and the fear of losing. Make sure that Lisa knows you've been interviewing other candidates, and that you need to get the decision finalized by a certain date (that's coming up very soon). The fear of losing the job if she takes too long to decide will get her to accept the job faster.

Use the word "you" as much as possible in the conversation, instead of "we" or "us." For example, "You are the best candidate. You will enjoy working at XYZ corporation. You will find that…"

The Need to Belong

Lisa is, at least in part, deciding whether to join the tribe that is your company or organization. If you make her feel that she belongs to your tribe, she'll be more likely to say yes to the job.

If you're not certain that Lisa will accept your offer, try to make the offer in person. If you can't do that, at least talk to Lisa by phone. You won't be able to use many of the strategies if you're corresponding via mail or email. A face-to-face meeting will allow you to use the most strategies.

Use bonding. Since you want to establish rapport with Lisa, try to do something together, synchronously, in order to bond. For example, see if the two of you can laugh at the same time about something. Do this early on in the meeting.

Watch your language. Speak confidently. Don't speak too fast or too slow. Communicate with passion, energy, and enthusiasm.

Imitate body movements and gestures. Try to imitate a few of Lisa's gestures and body movements during the interview to help build rapport.

Get Someone to Hire You as a Vendor

"I'm going to meet with a potential client. I'm hoping that the client will contract with us as a vendor for technology consulting services. I've set up a meeting with Scott, a VP at the company, to talk about why he should consider bringing us in as a vendor for their next technology project."

The best drivers in this situation are the same as for getting hired: Tricks of the Mind, Instincts, and the Need to Belong.

Tricks of the Mind

Activate System 1 thinking. You want Scott to use System 1 (that is, easy and intuitive) thinking as much as possible. As you talk about your company, the services you provide, and the clients you've done work for, stick to a clear, simple, coherent message. Simple is best.

Keep things easy to read. Because you want to keep System 1 operating, make sure any printed material you give Scott, such as a proposal or pricing, is in a simple, legible font and in a large enough type size so it's easy to read. Don't use a background color that makes the text hard to read.

Be the easy solution that makes ambiguity go away. We don't like ambiguity. Not knowing whom to bring in creates ambiguity and therefore an uncomfortable feeling. Make bringing you in the easy solution. Try not to cause any complications (for example, a lengthy, confusing contract that must go to the legal department).

Make your name easy to say. Remember that when your name is long or hard to pronounce, it erodes your credibility and makes what should seem easy (hiring you) now seem hard. If your business name is long and complicated, offer a shorter version or acronym.

Focus on the beginning and end of your meeting. Remember that people tend to forget the middle of a conversation, so make sure you open the conversation with important points, and that you end with important points.

Build rapport before you mention money. Make sure that you've built rapport with Scott before you start talking about money. Talking about money makes people independent and less collaborative.

Use anchoring to encourage Scott to purchase more products and services. Offer no more than three levels of service or bundles of products. Talk about the most expensive first to set the anchor point high.

Instincts

Use scarcity and fear of losing. Let Scott know that you're very busy, that you would like to work with him, and that you might be able to get him on the calendar if he decides quickly. The idea that Scott might lose the opportunity to work with you and your company because you're so busy will make you seem more appealing.

The Need to Belong

Use reciprocity. Offer Scott something that will make him indebted to you. Give him a free trial or anything that makes him feel that you've given him something of value or done him a favor.

If possible, meet in person. You won't be able to use many of the "Need to Belong" strategies if you're on the phone. The least effective way to communicate is via mail or email. You need to be able to talk directly to Scott. You want to at least speak to him remotely so you can use brain syncing between you.

Use bonding. Since you want to establish rapport with Scott, try to do something together, synchronously, in order to bond. For example, see if the two of you can laugh at the same time about something. Do this early on in the meeting.

Be a leader. You'll be more persuasive with Scott when he sees you as a leader. Talk first when you meet, but make it short—talking first (good thing) is not the same as dominating the entire conversation (bad thing).

Watch your language. Speak confidently. Don't speak too fast or too slow. Communicate with passion, energy, and enthusiasm.

Be mindful of your body language. Make sure to sit and stand up straight. Don't lean on furniture. Don't sit too far forward (conveys too much eagerness) or too far back (conveys disinterest). Practice some of your conversation in front of a mirror and make sure your hand gestures match your message. Remember to look Scott straight in the eyes sometimes and to smile slightly while talking.

Use similarity and attractiveness. Dress similar to how Scott dresses. Do your best to be as attractive as possible. Make sure you have a great haircut, good skincare, pressed clothes, shoes in good condition, and so on.

Imitate body movements and gestures. See if you can imitate a few of Scott's gestures and body movements to build rapport.

Drop names. Although indiscriminate and excessive name dropping can be annoying, it will help you a lot to mention companies you've worked with that Scott may recognize.

Get a reference or referral from a known person. Social validation is better than name dropping. Get a reference or referral from someone Scott knows personally, either inside or outside his company. Have him or her call or write to Scott, preferably *before* your interview.

Get Children to Practice Music

"We've heard about the benefits of having children learn music early. I've signed my daughter up for piano lessons. She likes the lessons, but she doesn't seem interested in practicing between lessons. How can I get her to practice more?"

When my children were growing up they took Suzuki music lessons (my daughter on piano and my son on violin). One of the tenets of Suzuki is that the student needs to practice music every day. But how do you get children to do that? There are many drivers to use, including the Power of Stories, Carrots and Sticks, Habits, the Need to Belong, and the Desire for Mastery.

Carrots and Sticks

We wanted to establish the behavior of practicing music every day, but before we could do that we had to get the children interested in playing the instrument at all. You might think that giving rewards to get people to practice would be an effective motivator, and indeed it was at the very beginning. The Suzuki teacher and I used carrots and sticks at the very beginning when the children were young (three years old). By using M&M's candy, colorful stickers, and praise, we were able to get the children interested in practice. But these strategies were quickly replaced with more powerful ones. Given what the research tells us about using extrinsic rewards, we might have discouraged practice eventually if all we had used were Carrots and Sticks strategies.

Habits

One of the best things we did to get the children to practice was to make it a daily habit. Initially we didn't practice every day. We would practice a few times a week. But that meant that every day someone had to decide whether today was a practice day or not. It became much easier when my children decided to see how many days in a row they could go without missing a practice. That meant that no one had to make a decision about whether to practice today or not. It was a day like any other. So of course they practiced—they practiced every day.

Everyone has routines, including children. My children would come home from school or from basketball practice, get a snack, and then practice their music. Practice time became just another daily activity, like getting dressed or brushing their teeth. Practicing music right before dinner became the habit.

It actually was much easier and went much more smoothly when it was a "do it every day" event, instead of a "do it some days" event.

The Power of Stories

I used story prompting to get stories started ("Since you are a piano player…"), and the children quickly developed self-personas around being musicians. They didn't need to do story editing, because they grew up with a story (I am a musician. I am someone who practices music). So that became a part of their self-personas and their self-stories. This is one of the advantages of working with young children—they will incorporate their activities into their self-personas. These are the same self-personas that we often are trying to change when we use strategies like story editing. In this case we have set a story early on that is positive and helpful, and that likely doesn't need to be changed in the future.

The Need to Belong

My children were part of the Suzuki music program. This is a worldwide system of teaching music. Suzuki teachers receive special training. They are certified as Suzuki instructors and take part in special Suzuki workshops all around the world. At our local music conservatory, where my children took lessons, there were annual Suzuki music concerts. My children attended a week of Suzuki instruction every summer at a university. You didn't just take music lessons, you became part of the Suzuki family. This meant that the children felt connected to other Suzuki students.

It was at our annual local Suzuki concert that my children first learned about the practice-every-day club. Some students were recognized for practicing every day for 30 days, 60 days, 90 days, 365 days, and more. This acted as social validation. "These children are doing this, maybe I should too?"

Another way we used the Need to Belong was by using nouns rather than verbs. Instead of saying, "My daughter plays the piano," we said, "My daughter is a pianist." This implied that she belonged to a group (of people who play piano).

The Desire for Mastery

I believe the most important driver for practicing every day was mastery. Learning a musical instrument is all about mastering a continuing and increasingly difficult set of physical, mental, and musical skills and knowledge. By hearing older students play, as well as listening to the musical recordings that we used in the Suzuki program, the children could always hear what they were aspiring toward. They would master one skill (for example, holding the wrist correctly for playing violin, or using the pedal during a piano piece), and then be ready for the next. Mastering and improving on a skill is a reward unto itself and keeps the student motivated.

Learning to play violin or piano is challenging but not impossible, and the constant challenge keeps students motivated. It's like striving to reach the next level in a game.

Students get lots of feedback when they take music lessons, and this feedback stimulates the desire for mastery. Because the students can see and feel that they're progressing in mastery when they practice every day, it keeps them practicing.

Get Customers to Be Evangelists

"I know that getting our customers to rave about our company and its products and services is one of the best ways to grow our business, but how do we get customers to do this?"

We'll assume that you have a great product or service, and that what you want is for existing, happy customers to take the next step and become evangelists. Let's look at what turns a satisfied customer into an evangelist. People become evangelists when

- They identify as a member of the tribe of people who love your products ("I'm an Apple person," "I'm a Pepsi person").
- They want to appear smart and in the know about the field ("I'm fashion forward," "I'm savvy about new technologies").
- They feel that your product or service will be useful, helpful, or enjoyable for others in their tribe.

The best drivers to use are Carrots and Sticks, the Power of Stories, and the Need to Belong.

Carrots and Sticks

More important than giving an actual reward is that you have some kind of loyalty program for your customers. You probably don't actually need Carrots and Sticks, but it can't hurt to reward your favorite customers for their loyalty. More important than the reward is that by being a "frequent flyer" type of member, they are joining your "club" and thereby stating that they are a frequent customer.

The Need to Belong

When you offer your customers the sense that they're part of a group (people who love what you offer), it will be easy to get them to want to belong to that group.

Use social validation. When your customers know that there are many other people who are also fans of your company and its products or services, they'll be more likely to become evangelists too.

Provide a platform for evangelists to be heard by other customers. Things go viral when there's strong emotional content, passion, and a good story. When you have a few passionate customers who are willing to talk about their story with your company, make it easy to get that story out there. When you have a few evangelists, they'll encourage others to become evangelists.

Use reciprocity. Give your customers small perks and gifts and they'll return the favor (by telling others how great you are).

Use nouns. Refer to your customers using nouns rather than verbs, so they'll be encouraged to do the same: "You are a Pepsi drinker," rather than "You drink Pepsi." Nouns encourage the feeling of being a member of a group.

The Power of Stories

Encourage your customers to make a public commitment. When someone writes a positive review of your product or service, he has essentially publicly committed to it. Committing to it publicly will make people more likely to become evangelists.

Share others' stories. When your customers read about other customers who are evangelists, it encourages them to make the leap from happy customer to evangelist.

Get People to Vote

"How do you get people to vote: Not to vote for a particular candidate, but just to go to the polls and actually vote?"

The best drivers to use are Tricks of the Mind, the Need to Belong, and the Power of Stories.

Tricks of the Mind

Get people to ask themselves a "Will I…" question. See if you can get people to say to themselves, or write down, "Will I be a voter in this election?" People who ask themselves "Will I" questions are more likely to take action.

The Need to Belong

Use nouns. When you talk to people, use the phrase "I am a voter," or the question "Are you a voter?" rather than a verb ("I vote," or "Are you going to vote?"). Using a noun implies belonging to a group (of voters) and increases the likelihood that they'll vote.

Use social validation. Provide information on others voting. Let them know how many other people are voting, for example, "In elections like this, over 70 percent of eligible people vote."

Use similarity and attractiveness. Show images of other people voting that are attractive and/or similar to the people that you are trying to get to go vote.

Have someone familiar do the asking. People will be more likely to vote when someone they know encourages them to do so.

The Power of Stories

Tie voting to an existing persona. Let's say you have a group of people who care about a certain issue, for example, the environment. Tie voting in the upcoming election to caring for the environment. Tell a story where the logical conclusion is that when you care about the environment, you would, of course, be a voter.

Get a smaller commitment first. When the people you're trying to influence are not currently voters and don't think of themselves that way, see if you can get them to take a small action first; for instance, get them to state (as publicly as possible) that they're interested in the upcoming election, or that they like a particular candidate. Taking this small action first will make a slight change in their self-personas. Instead of "I'm someone who isn't that interested in politics," they will adopt the persona of "I'm someone who cares about the upcoming election." Once they've taken that step, it's a smaller step to actually go vote, since voting is consistent with the new persona.

Get people to make a public commitment. For example, ask them to say where their polling place is located. Stating "I vote at the school in my neighborhood," or "I vote at the city offices on Third Avenue," makes them more likely to vote.

Go a step further than just asking people to make a commitment publicly. Ask them to write down something about the voting. This might be "I'm going to go vote on November 3," or "I'm going to be a voter at the Village Hall on Third Avenue on November 3," or even "I am a voter." When possible ask them to write this out longhand rather than type it. Writing something longhand changes where and how it is stored in the brain, and makes it more likely that it will happen.

Get People to Live a Healthier Lifestyle

"I'm concerned about my mom (Elizabeth). She's always been a fairly healthy person, but now she's getting older and I've noticed that she isn't eating healthy food anymore, and has stopped exercising. Is there anything I can do to get her to live a healthier lifestyle?"

There are many drivers you can use to get someone to consider and implement a healthier lifestyle, including Habits, Tricks of the Mind, Carrots and Sticks, Instincts, the Need to Belong, and the Power of Stories.

Habits

Help Elizabeth set up new habits that are linked to old habits. Since a lot of the things we do throughout the day are habitual, you can help Elizabeth eat healthier and exercise more by looking at her existing habits and connecting new, healthier habits to the existing ones. Don't concentrate on her unhealthy habits. Instead, look at the habits that are neutral (going to the store, feeding the dog) and attach new, healthy habits to those. For example, every time she feeds the dog she could get ready to go out for a walk, and as soon as the dog is done eating they could go for a 20-minute walk together. Every time she gets ready to go grocery shopping she could make a list of healthy things to eat and put them on the grocery list.

Tricks of the Mind

Start by talking to Elizabeth about something she already knows and agrees with. You want to get around any confirmation biases (we pay attention only to things that fit what we already believe) and avoid making her defensive. Begin your conversation with her by talking about something she already knows and agrees with. I can't tell you exactly what that is because I don't know her like you do. If you know that she thinks and agrees that being healthy is important, start there. If she knows that her recent lifestyle choices leave something to be desired, start there. Start with something she already knows and agrees with, then you can move on to discuss ideas she may not agree with.

Once you've started the conversation with something that Elizabeth knows and agrees with, introduce cognitive dissonance. You might begin with some statistics on health: women past middle age who are inactive (less than an hour of exercise a week) have double the risk of dying from a cardiovascular event compared to women who exercise more. Elizabeth wants to be healthy and live a long life, but now she has to face that she's in the group that has double the risk. This sets up cognitive dissonance. This will make her uncomfortable.

Provide an easy solution to make the dissonance go away. When you provide an answer or solution at the moment of cognitive dissonance that takes the dissonance away, she'll be more likely to take action. For example, you could say, "How about we start going to the gym together three times a week?"

Instincts

Invoke the fear of losing to motivate Elizabeth to act. If she's afraid of losing her health, years off her life, or mobility, you can use these ideas to help propel her to action.

Suggest a limited number of choices. Don't overwhelm her with ten different things she could and should change. Too many choices will lead her to not choose at all. Instead, give her just a few—no more than three or four—suggestions of what she could do differently.

Carrots and Sticks

Give a reward for the behavior you want to encourage. Figure out what would act as a reinforcer for your mom and consider applying that when she does something that encourages a healthy lifestyle. For example, let's say that spending time with you is a reward for her. When she goes to the gym with you, take her out for coffee and conversation immediately after the gym session.

The Need to Belong

Use social validation. When you know that some of Elizabeth's friends or celebrities she looks up to have a healthy lifestyle, talk about those people with her.

Connect her with other active people. When she feels part of a group, she'll be more likely to continue with the activities.

Use nouns instead of verbs in order to get her to feel that she's part of a healthy lifestyle group. Try saying, "It's great to see that you've become such a swimmer," instead of "It's great to see you swimming."

The Power of Stories

Share stories of other people who have healthy lifestyles. When Elizabeth hears about others who are modeling the behavior you hope she will embrace, she may create a new story for herself.

If she has a self-persona that's consistent with a healthy lifestyle, ask her to do something that matches that self-persona: "I know you like to stay active. I was thinking maybe you would like to go on a bike ride with me on Sunday."

If her current self-persona is *not* consistent with a healthy lifestyle, ask her to do something very small that is inconsistent with her current lifestyle. For example, "Let's go for a short walk together today." Once she takes an action that is inconsistent with her current self-persona, it will be easier for her to start building a new self-persona that fits with the new activities.

Get People to Use Checklists

"I work at a company that teaches seminars and workshops. We have a lot of errors with shipping out course materials. It happens too often that when the instructor arrives at a client site to teach and opens up the boxes something is missing. Sometimes it's that there aren't enough student manuals, or the nametags are missing. I'd like to have the staff fill out a checklist before the boxes go out. How can we get the people who work in this department to use a checklist?"

The best drivers for getting people to do something like use a checklist are Habits, Tricks of the Mind, the Need to Belong, and the Power of Stories.

Habits

Connect the use of a checklist to an existing habit. Analyze the current habits of the staff. What do they do without thinking? Take one of those existing habits and make filling out the new checklist something they do at the beginning or end of the existing habit. For example, perhaps every time they start packing for a new workshop they fill out a shipping form for where the boxes are going to. Take that habit and attach filling out the checklist at the same time.

Tricks of the Mind

Use a heavy clipboard. You can trigger embodied cognition by using something heavy for the checklist. When you attach the checklist to a heavy clipboard, it has more weight and will be seen as more important.

The Need to Belong

Make the use of the checklist a team event. People will be more likely to use it when they feel that it's for the team, not just an individual. When possible, report statistics on the team's use of the checklist.

Use brain syncing. When you introduce the checklist, do so in person or at least over the phone. Don't use written communication alone. You want their brains to sync with the person who's talking about the checklist.

Use imitation. When you want people to use the checklist, make sure you use it too, since people will imitate you.

Use passion. People are more likely to do something when it's presented to them in an exciting way. You might not think a checklist could be exciting, but when it results in 50 percent fewer errors, you can probably find an instructor who could talk about that in a very passionate way.

Use social validation. When you know of other companies, departments, or individuals that are using the same or similar checklists, talk about them. Better yet, get one or more of those people to talk to your team about how checklists have helped them.

The Power of Stories

Tie the checklist into an existing self-persona. If the people on your team think of themselves as careful, conscientious people, tie that in to the checklist: "I know that you're a careful person. This checklist will help you be careful."

If they don't have a self-persona that would use a checklist, you'll need to change the self-persona. Have them start with a smaller task than using the whole checklist. Have them do one thing that will help them think of themselves as careful people. For example, ask them to do one activity on the checklist for a week before introducing the whole checklist ("count the number of manuals before you put them in the box and make sure it's the same number as the number of students attending").

Have them literally check off each item on the checklist, sign the list, and include it in the shipping box each time they complete it. Having people write by hand and sign the form increases their commitment.

Get People to Recycle

"I work in city government. How can we get people to do more recycling rather than just throwing things into the trash?"

The best drivers to get people to do more recycling are Tricks of the Mind, Habits, the Need to Belong, and the Power of Stories.

Tricks of the Mind

When you want people to make a quick decision at the point when they're about to throw something away, you want to engage System 1 thinking. Make things easy and effortless. Have special recycling bins that are a different size, shape, and color. Use a large and easy-to-read font to indicate which bins are for what.

If you're trying to persuade people who don't currently recycle and aren't all that interested in changing their behavior, start by telling them something they already agree with. For example, tell them, "Taking out the trash is not the most fun activity, is it!" Next you can introduce the idea of recycling.

Introduce cognitive dissonance. Show a picture of a huge landfill, or give some statistics about garbage. Then provide them with an easy solution (recycling).

Get them to ask themselves a "Will I" question. For example, "Will I recycle this year?"

Invoke a metaphor that implies that they have the power to take action. For example, "We're clogging our neighborhood with our garbage, but you can clean it out with recycling."

Habits

Encourage people to analyze their habit of throwing things away, and figure out new anchors. For example, what if they purchased special bags for recycling every time they purchased garbage bags? Or perhaps they could move the basket where they put their mail each day to a location nearer to the paper recycling bin.

The Need to Belong

Get people to feel connected. Invoke the sense of a neighborhood (whether that's a part of a town, an entire town, a large city, or an entire country) to make them feel that they're in this together. For example, use messaging about how reducing what goes into a landfill affects the group.

Use the power of others' opinions. Assuming that a significant number or percentage of people are already recycling, give people that information: "65 percent of the people in our city regularly recycle."

When possible, do what the energy companies did in the Allcott research that we covered in Chapter 2, "The Need to Belong." Send people information that compares their recycling behavior with that of their neighbors.

The Power of Stories

Tie the recycling behavior into a current self-persona. For example, people who care about their neighborhoods also care about recycling.

For people who don't already have self-personas that tie into recycling, ask them to take a small action first. Rather than expecting them to fully embrace recycling, ask them to place a related bumper sticker on their car or put a related button on their backpack. Then come back and ask them to commit to recycling.

Ask people to publicly commit. For example, ask them to sign their names to a list of people who have agreed to recycle in the neighborhood.

Get Customers to Be Actively Involved

"At my company we believe that getting customers actively involved with us is key to keeping their loyalty to our brand. My job is to try and get people to engage with our company. We want people to give us feedback, engage in forums, and such. We ask for feedback, but we don't get much. How can we get people more actively involved?"

The best drivers to use in this situation are Carrots and Sticks, the Need to Belong, the Power of Stories, and the Desire for Mastery.

Carrots and Sticks

Reward people for participating. Figure out what would be reinforcing for your customers, and reward them when they participate in being actively involved. The most obvious idea is to give them coupons for your products and services, but there are other rewards as well. You might want to recognize the customers who give the most useful feedback with a badge that appears next to their name or photo online. Recognition can be a powerful reinforcer. Or provide them with expanded access to customer support, or an invitation to join a monthly phone call with the CEO.

The Need to Belong

Put together a community of customers who give feedback. Rather than asking customers to complete a survey, or just encouraging them to comment, put together a customer feedback group. Consider making the group "elite." For example, require them to do certain things (products or services to buy, forums to participate in) before they're invited to become part of the special customer participation group.

Allow the members of the group to communicate with one another, not just with your company. People will participate more when they feel that they're actually part of a group.

Use reciprocity. Give people something, then ask them to give you feedback, fill out a survey, or perform some other action. People are more likely to give you feedback and to participate when doing so helps them discharge a feeling of indebtedness.

The Power of Stories

Encourage people to use stories to give you feedback. Show them others' stories and encourage them to write their own.

Tie participation into an existing persona. For example, "Since you're someone who likes to help others, please consider joining our forum. Your feedback will help other people understand whether our product is right for them."

Encourage people to publicly commit; don't allow people to participate anonymously. Once they've publicly responded, they'll be more likely to do so again.

The Desire for Mastery

Offer to teach people skills as part of their giving feedback. Would they like to learn how a focus group works? Would they like to learn how to participate in market research? These might be skills they could use elsewhere.

Give people feedback on their feedback. Show them how they can give even more valuable feedback than they are already. Teach them how to be active participants.

Provide opportunities for more involved feedback. You might think that a short, easy survey is the best way to get feedback, and that's true when you want to get responses from as many people as possible. But when what you want is deeper involvement from a subset of people, consider making the feedback process challenging. I'm not suggesting that you create a survey that's hard to fill out, but consider doing more than a survey. Invite people to be part of your beta testing team or to participate in one-on-one user testing sessions. People like a challenge.

Get People to See the Other Side

"How can you get people to consider the other side of an argument, and even dare to imagine that you aren't an idiot just for having a different opinion?"

The best drivers to use to get people to see another point of view are Instincts, the Need to Belong, Tricks of the Mind, and the Power of Stories.

Instincts

We often react the way we do because we're afraid. It's possible that, unconsciously, your opinion or point of view is frightening to others.

Let's say that you've started a new job at a company that makes industrial equipment. You want the company to implement more automation. You think this is standard best practice, and are surprised that some people at the company are strongly opposed to your idea. You've tried to talk to them about the advantages of automation, but they tune you out.

You may not realize that some people are afraid of your idea. You think implementing automation has few negatives, and that the positives far outweigh the negatives. They think that you're trying to take over and impose new ideas that will eventually lead to loss of jobs, maybe even their own jobs.

When you get strong resistance to something, look at the difference of opinion and see if something about what you're saying is causing people to be afraid of losing something. If so, make note of it, as you'll use it in the next driver, Tricks of the Mind.

Tricks of the Mind

Start with something that everyone agrees with. When people are so resistant that they won't even listen to your point of view, they may be reacting instantly with System 1 thinking and the confirmation bias. They're filtering out what you're saying because it doesn't match what they believe.

Instead of pushing your ideas more strongly, talk about something you know that they *do* believe and something you can agree on. For example, say the group you're talking to is opposed to automation, but everyone agrees that it would be good to fulfill customer orders more quickly. Back off talking about automation from the start. Instead start with what everyone can agree on.

Even better, use the idea that you identified as being what people are afraid of. If the fear is loss of jobs, start by talking about how important it is to retain good jobs for people. By starting with something that people agree with, and something that speaks to their fear, you allow people to listen to you without filtering.

Use cognitive dissonance to make people feel uncomfortable. Once you have them listening to you, introduce an idea, a fact, data, or a statistic that produces cognitive dissonance. For example, "Did you know that automation creates more jobs than it eliminates?" When you set up cognitive dissonance, System 1 thinking stops and System 2 (logical, analytical thinking) takes over.

At that point there will be less automatic filtering, and your new ideas will be able to get through.

The Need to Belong

Have someone that people know do the talking. When you're new to the company, you might not be the best person to do the talking. People will listen to and be more persuaded by someone they know.

Be as similar as possible. The more you look like them and act like them, the more similar you are to them. And the more similar you are, the more likely it is that they'll listen to you.

Use reciprocity. When you do something for someone, he'll be indebted to you. When he can relieve the debt by listening to you for a few minutes, he'll opt to do that. So before you make your pitch, do something for the person or people you want to listen to you. Even something as simple as bringing snacks to the meeting can make a difference. You've given the group something (food) and now they need to give something back to you (hearing your ideas).

The Power of Stories

Use stories. If you want people to listen to your side of the story, you need to get them to feel empathetic. The best way to get them to feel empathetic is to tell a story. Even when you have facts and figures to report or share, provide them inside of, or in addition to, one or more stories. For example, "You're all familiar with the XYZ plant in Baltimore, right? I was speaking with the plant manager there just last month. He told me that…"

Tie your idea into an existing self-persona. For example, "Since you're someone who likes to do everything you can to improve efficiency…"

Ask for a small commitment. Before you ask the group to support a huge automation project, try to get them to commit to a small research project: "I know you have many questions that haven't been resolved yet, so I'm not asking you to agree to move forward with a large automation project. Would you be willing to join me in a tour of the plant in Savannah? They're in the process of doing some automation, and I thought we could talk to them and see what their experience has been." Once they've taken the tour and thus made a small commitment to the idea of automation, they'll have a new self-persona of "I'm someone who is interested in automation."

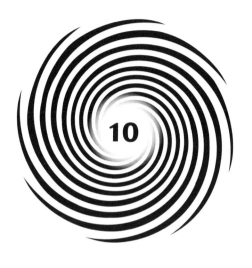

The Strategy List

The Need To Belong

Strategy 1: Get people to feel connected to others and they will work harder.

Strategy 2: When you ask for something, use nouns to invoke group identity rather than verbs.

Strategy 3: To get people to do something, show them that others are already doing it.

Strategy 4: It matters who does the asking. It's most effective when the asking is done by a friend, someone attractive, or someone similar to those being asked.

Strategy 5: Before you try to get people to do stuff, do something for them so they feel the need to reciprocate.

Strategy 6: Ask for more than you really want. When you get turned down, ask for what you really want.

Strategy 7: To get people to do something, make sure you're doing it first (because they will imitate you).

Strategy 8: To build rapport, imitate others' body positions and gestures. This builds connectedness and makes them more likely to do what you ask of them.

Strategy 9: To get people to do something, show that you're passionate about what you're asking them to do.

Strategy 10: To make something go viral, use strong emotional content, passion, and a good story to communicate the idea or the call to action.

Strategy 11: To get people to do something, first bond them together as a group with some kind of laughter or synchronous behavior.

Strategy 12: To get people to trust you, first show them that you trust them. When they trust you, they'll be more likely to do what you ask them to.

Strategy 13: To get people to do something, sync your communication directly with their brains. They need to hear your voice.

Strategy 14: Use competition only with a small number (fewer than 10) of competitors.

Strategy 15: Don't mix men and women in a competition.

Strategy 16: People are more likely to do what you want them to do when they consider you a leader. To be seen as a leader, you must show confidence via your body posture and stance.

Strategy 17: To be persuasive, your hand gestures must match what you're saying.

Strategy 18: You'll be more persuasive when you look directly at a person and use a slight smile.

Strategy 19: To excite someone to do something, communicate with energy and enthusiasm.

Strategy 20: To get people to do stuff, you must either dress like them to make use of similarity or dress a notch above them to make use of authority.

Strategy 21: Talk first and you will be seen as the leader. When you're the leader, you'll be more likely to get people to do stuff.

Habits

Strategy 22: To get people to do something automatically for a long time, get them to create a new habit or change an existing one.

Strategy 23: To get someone to create a new habit, figure out a cue and a reward.

Strategy 24: To encourage the creation of a habit, break the desired behavior into small steps.

Strategy 25: To get people to start a new habit, make it as easy as possible and eliminate all decision making except the decision to start the routine. All other steps should happen as automatically as possible.

Strategy 26: To get people to stick with the new routine and the new habit, show results and progress. Habits need lots of feedback on what is happening.

Strategy 27: To create a new habit, anchor it to an existing habit.

Strategy 28: Use new habit creation when you want people to do something that is relatively small, yet you want them to do it unconsciously and automatically.

The Power of Stories

Strategy 29: People are more likely to do what you ask of them when you communicate your supporting information and data in the form of a story.

Strategy 30: When you get people to change their own persona stories, they'll change their behaviors.

Strategy 31: Before you ask people to do something, activate a persona that's connected to what you want them to do.

Strategy 32: When you introduce a small crack in an existing persona, you'll change the persona over time. When you change the persona, you can then change the behavior.

Strategy 33: To get people to do something, use an existing persona and anchor a new—but related—persona to it.

Strategy 34: To change a persona, get people to take one small action that is inconsistent with their current persona.

Strategy 35: When you get people to commit publicly, it's easier to get them to do stuff.

Strategy 36: Don't pay people for their commitments.

Strategy 37: When people write their commitments longhand, they are more committed.

Strategy 38: Expose people to the stories of others so they'll be encouraged to create new stories for themselves.

Carrots and Sticks

Strategy 39: Once people become conditioned to do something, you can pair a new stimulus to the behavior you want and get people to respond automatically.

Strategy 40: It's not enough to just give a reward. You need to decide which type of schedule to use if you want the reward to be effective in getting people to do stuff.

Strategy 41: When you're trying to establish a new behavior, give a reward every time the person does the behavior (continuous reinforcement).

Strategy 42: Once a behavior is established with continuous reinforcement, switch to a different reward schedule to keep the behavior going.

Strategy 43: When you want a behavior to stick, give rewards on a variable ratio schedule.

Strategy 44: Use a variable interval schedule when you don't need a lot of a certain behavior; you simply want to see the behavior steadily and regularly.

Strategy 45: When you use a fixed ratio schedule, you'll get a burst of behavior, but it will drop off after the reward.

Strategy 46: When you use a fixed ratio schedule, people will be most motivated when you show them how much is left to reach the goal—not just how far they've come.

Strategy 47: Avoid giving rewards based on a fixed time interval. This schedule of reinforcement is less effective than other intervals.

Strategy 48: When you can't reward a behavior because it doesn't exist, use shaping to kick-start the behavior.

Strategy 49: Choose a reward that the person really wants. Otherwise, rewards don't work.

Strategy 50: When you provide rewards, give them immediately after the behavior (according to the schedule you're using).

Strategy 51: When you provide rewards, give them *after* the behavior, not *before* the behavior.

Strategy 52: You can use negative reinforcement to get people to do stuff. Figure out what someone *doesn't* want and remove it for them as a type of "reward."

Strategy 53: Reward the behavior you want and ignore the behavior you don't want. Punishment is less effective than rewards.

Instincts

Strategy 54: To grab attention, use messages and photos of dangerous events.

Strategy 55: To get people to remember you, your brand, or your message, use photos or wording that inspire fear.

Strategy 56: To get people to take immediate action, use messages of fear and death.

Strategy 57: Understand that people are more motivated by the possibility of loss than the possibility of gain.

Strategy 58: Don't rely on people to self-report why they prefer one choice over another.

Strategy 59: When you want people to crave something, let them try it first. Once they've tried it, they won't want to lose it.

Strategy 60: When you want people to value your product or service, make it scarce or difficult to get.

Strategy 61: When you want people to try something new, engage them when they're in a good mood or help them get into a good mood by showing a fun or funny video.

Strategy 62: When you want people to try something new, make sure they're feeling safe and comfortable.

Strategy 63: When you want people to stick with what's familiar, avoid putting them in a good mood.

Strategy 64: When you want people to stick with their usual choice and not try something new, use messaging that invokes the fear of loss.

Strategy 65: When you give people choices, you give them control—and people love to have control.

Strategy 66: Limit the number of choices to three or four. When you provide too many choices, people won't choose anything at all.

Strategy 67: When you want people to participate, make them feel safe.

Strategy 68: To grab attention, use novelty. Once you have people's attention, give them your message.

Strategy 69: Influence people to desire more by giving them a limited amount of information.

Strategy 70: When you want undivided attention, make the stimulus unpredictable and include an auditory or visual alert.

Strategy 71: To grab attention, use actual food, the smell of food, or even a picture of food.

Strategy 72: To grab attention and affect decision making, use any hint of sex—as long as the use of sex is appropriate.

The Desire for Mastery

Strategy 73: When you want people to do something complicated, something that requires learning new skills or gaining a new body of knowledge, use the desire for mastery. If not, then reinforcements may be the better option.

Strategy 74: To get people to do stuff over the long term, engage their desire for mastery—don't just give them cash or other rewards.

Strategy 75: When you make people feel that only members of an elite group can do a certain task, they'll be more motivated to master the task.

Strategy 76: When you make a task seem challenging (but not impossible), people will be motivated to pursue it.

Strategy 77: When you provide people with autonomy, they feel a stronger desire for mastery and thus are more motivated.

Strategy 78: When you make people struggle, at least a little bit, it increases their sense of mastery and thereby increases their level of motivation.

Strategy 79: Provide people with opportunities to make mistakes.

Strategy 80: Give feedback to help people learn from their mistakes, but don't interrupt their work in order to do so.

Strategy 81: When you give feedback, provide a short elaboration.

Strategy 82: Pick the right time to give feedback.

Strategy 83: When you use feedback to increase the desire for mastery, keep the feedback objective and don't include praise.

Strategy 84: When you induce a flow state, people will work longer and harder.

Strategy 85: To keep a flow state going, give people control over their actions during the activity.

Strategy 86: To keep a flow state going, don't interrupt people.

Strategy 87: To keep the flow state going, make sure the task is challenging but not impossible.

Tricks of the Mind

Strategy 88: When you want people to make a quick decision, make the thinking easy for them.

Strategy 89: When you want people to think things through, make the thinking more difficult for them.

Strategy 90: When you want people to respond quickly, make a simple request that doesn't require them to think.

Strategy 91: When you use a simple, coherent story, you make it more likely that people will make a decision or take an action.

Strategy 92: When you want people to act independently, make a reference to money.

Strategy 93: When you want people to work with others or help others, *don't* refer to money.

Strategy 94: When you want people to obey authority, use messages of death.

Strategy 95: When you want people to follow the social norms of the group they identify with, use messages of death.

Strategy 96: When you want people to be charitable to people within their community, use messages of death.

Strategy 97: When you want people to be sympathetic or charitable to people outside their community, *avoid* messages of death.

Strategy 98: When you want people to accept a high number, anchor with a high number.

Strategy 99: When you want people to accept a low number, anchor with a low number.

Strategy 100: To influence how people perceive prices and make numerical estimates, use an arbitrary number to act as an anchor.

Strategy 101: When you want people to choose a higher level of product or service, start your list with the highest level of service and the highest price.

Strategy 102: When you want people to stay close to your initial anchor price, use a very specific anchor.

Strategy 103: When you want people to consider prices that are different than your initial anchor price, use a less specific anchor.

Strategy 104: When you want people to think of a product or idea in a positive way, make that product or idea familiar to them.

Strategy 105: When you want people to think what you have is good and true, keep the message simple and expose them to it five to seven times.

Strategy 106: When you want people to think that a similar event is likely to happen again, ask them right after the first event occurs.

Strategy 107: When you want people to *underestimate* the likelihood of an event occurring, ask them about a similar event that *hasn't* occurred recently.

Strategy 108: When you want people to *overestimate* the likelihood of an event occurring, ask them about a similar event that *has* occurred recently.

Strategy 109: When you want people to respond quickly to what they're reading, make it easy to read.

Strategy 110: When you want people to use more thought or analysis before responding to what they read, make it more difficult to read.

Strategy 111: When you want people to make quick decisions without thinking, don't do anything surprising.

Strategy 112: When you want people to think more carefully, do something unexpected.

Strategy 113: When trying to break through a confirmation bias, start by telling people something they already know and agree with.

Strategy 114: When trying to break through a confirmation bias, use cognitive dissonance to make people uncomfortable for a moment.

Strategy 115: Once you establish cognitive dissonance, provide an answer or solution that relieves people's discomfort. You'll be a hero for making them comfortable while also solving the problem, and you will therefore break through the confirmation bias.

Strategy 116: To propel people to action, use ambiguity and uncertainty.

Strategy 117: To make ambiguity go away, provide an easy solution that resolves the ambiguity.

Strategy 118: To get people to truly grasp what you're telling them, build in breaks at least every 20 minutes.

Strategy 119: When you want to come across as smart or when you simply want to make a point, use a quote that rhymes.

Strategy 120: To establish credibility with your audience, choose a product or service name that's easy to pronounce.

Strategy 121: When you want people to remember something, reduce the amount of sensory input and stress they experience.

Strategy 122: When you want people to remember something, repeat their exposure to it and have them actively repeat the information.

Strategy 123: When you want people to remember something, present that "something" at the beginning or end of an event, not in the middle.

Strategy 124: When you want people to remember what you have to say, use concrete words rather than abstract ones.

Strategy 125: To get people to do stuff, get to know them and their schemas so you can tailor your strategy to fit how they look at the world.

Strategy 126: Closely examine your assumptions about schemas—we tend to think our schemas are the same as those of the people we're interacting with, but our schemas might be different.

Strategy 127: When you can get people to ask themselves a question beginning with "Will I...," you're more likely to get them to act on the statement.

Strategy 128: Carefully choose the metaphors you use to describe a situation to others. The metaphor frames the question and affects the solution and outcome.

Strategy 129: To get people to take an action, use their tendency to act on impulse.

Strategy 130: To encourage impulsive action, make your request specific, simple, and quick.

Strategy 131: When you want people to spend more money, first ask them to spend more of their time.

Strategy 132: Sell people on the experience. They'll spend more money on an experience than they will on an item.

Strategy 133: Accept the fact that people's minds are wandering at least a third of the time and use the strategies in this book to get their attention.

Strategy 134: When you want people to solve problems, especially creatively, let them stop thinking.

Strategy 135: To maximize problem-solving skills, build in nonstructured mind wandering time.

Strategy 136: When you want people to feel less regretful, offer them fewer choices.

Strategy 137: When you want people to take action, engage them while they're feeling regret.

Strategy 138: When you want people to interact smoothly and flexibly, use soft objects and smooth fabrics.

Strategy 139: When you want people to perceive that what you're saying is important, have them hold something heavy.

Strategy 140: When you want people to react to you warmly, don't let them hold cold drinks. Give them a cup of something hot.

APPENDIX A

References

Aaker, Jennifer, Andy Smith, Dan Ariely, Chip Heath, and Carlye Adler. 2010. *The Dragonfly Effect: Quick, Effective, and Powerful Ways to Use Social Media to Drive Social Change.* San Francisco: Jossey-Bass.

Ackerman, Joshua M., Christopher Nocera, and John Bargh. 2010. "Incidental haptic sensations influence social judgments and decisions." *Science* 328(5986): 1712–15. doi: 10.1126/science.1189993.

Allcott, H. 2011. "Social norms and energy conservation," *Journal of Public Economics.* doi: 10.1016/j.jpubeco.2011.03.003.

Anderson, Cameron, and Gavin Kilduff. 2009. "Why do dominant personalities attain influence in face-to-face groups? The competence-signaling effects of trait dominance." *Journal of Personality and Social Psychology* 96(2): 491–503.

Ariely, Dan. 2009. *Predictably Irrational: The Hidden Forces that Shape Our Decisions.* New York: HarperCollins.

Ariely, Dan, George Loewenstein, and Drazen Prelec. 2003. "Coherent arbitrariness: Stable demand curves without stable preferences." *Quarterly Journal of Economics* 118(1): 73–105.

Bechara, Antoine, H. Damasio, D. Tranel, and A. Damasio. 1997. "Deciding advantageously before knowing the advantageous strategy." *Science* 275(5304): 1293–95. doi: 10.1126/science.275.5304.1293.

Berger, Jonah, and Katherine L. Milkman. 2012. "What makes online content viral?" *Journal of Marketing Research* 49(2), 192–205. doi: 10.1509/jmr.10.0353.

Berridge, Kent, and T. Robinson. 1998. "What is the role of dopamine in reward: Hedonic impact, reward learning, or incentive salience?" *Brain Research Reviews* 28(3): 309–69.

Bickman, L. 1974. "The social power of a uniform." *Journal of Applied Social Psychology* 4(1): 47–61. doi: 10.1111/j.1559-1816.1974.tb02599.x.

Briñol, Pablo, R. E. Petty, and B. Wagner. 2009. "Body posture effects on self-evaluation: A self-validation approach." *European Journal of Social Psychology* 39(6): 1053–64. doi: 10.1002/ejsp.607.

Chaiken, Shelly. 1979. "Communicator physical attractiveness and persuasion." *Journal of Personality and Social Psychology* 37(8): 1387–97. doi: 10.1037/0022-3514.37.8.1387.

Chartrand, Tanya L., and John Bargh. 1999. "The chameleon effect: The perception-behavior link and social interaction." *Journal of Personality and Social Psychology 76*(6): 893–910.

Christoff, Kalina, A. M. Gordon, J. Smallwood, R. Smith, and J. Schooler. 2009. "Experience sampling during fMRI reveals default network and executive system contributions to mind wandering." *Proceedings of the National Academy of the Sciences 106*(21): 8719–24.

Cialdini, Robert. 2006. *Influence: The Psychology of Persuasion*. New York: HarperCollins.

Cialdini, R. B., J. E. Vincent, S. K. Lewis, J. Catalan, D. Wheeler, and B. L. Darby. 1975. "A reciprocal concessions procedure for inducing compliance: The door-in-the-face technique." *Journal of Personality and Social Psychology 31*(2), 206–15. doi: 10.1037/h0076284.

Csikszentmihalyi, Mihaly. 2008. *Flow: The Psychology of Optimal Experience*. New York: Harper.

Damasio, Antonio. 1994. *Descartes' Error: Emotion, Reason, and the Human Brain*. New York: Penguin.

Deutsch, Morton, and Harold B. Gerard. 1955. "A study of normative and informational social influences upon individual judgment." *The Journal of Abnormal and Social Psychology 51*(3): 629–36. doi: 10.1037/h0046408.

De Vries, Marieke, R. Holland, and C. Witteman. 2008. "Fitting decisions: Mood and intuitive versus deliberative decision strategies." *Cognition and Emotion 22*(5): 931–43. doi: 10.1080/02699930701552580.

DiSalvo, David. 2011. *What Makes Your Brain Happy and Why You Should Do the Opposite*. Amherst, New York: Prometheus Books.

Duhigg, Charles. 2012. *The Power of Habit: Why We Do What We Do in Life and Business*. New York: Random House.

Efran, M. G., and E.W.J Patterson. 1974. "Voters vote beautiful: The effect of physical appearance on a national election." *Canadian Journal of Behavioural Science, 6*(4): 352–56.

Frederick, Shane. 2005. "Cognitive reflection and decision making." *Journal of Economic Perspectives 19*(4): 25–42. doi: 10.1257/089533005775196732.

Freedman, Jonathan L., and Scott C. Fraser. 1966. "Compliance without pressure: The foot-in-the-door technique." *Journal of Personality and Social Psychology, 4*(2): 195–202.

Garcia, S., and A. Tor. 2009. "The N-effect: More competitors, less competition." *Psychological Science 20*(7): 871–77. doi: 10.1111/j.1467-9280.2009.02385.x.

Gilbert, D. T., C. K. Morewedge, J. L. Risen, and T. D. Wilson. 2004. "Looking forward to looking backward: The misprediction of regret." *Psychological Science 15*(5): 346–50.

Gilbert, D. T., and J.E.J. Ebert. 2002. "Decisions and revisions: The affective forecasting of changeable outcomes." *Journal of Personality and Social Psychology 82*(4): 503–14.

Gneezy, Uri, Muriel Niederle, and Aldo Rustichini. 2003. "Performance in competitive environments: Gender differences." *Quarterly Journal of Economics 118*(3): 1049–74. doi: 10.1162/00335530360698496.

Gneezy, Uri, and Aldo Rustichini. 2000. "A fine is a price." *Journal of Legal Studies 29*(1), 1–17.

Goman, Carol Kinsey. 2011. *The Silent Language of Leaders: How Body Language Can Help—or Hurt—How You Lead*. San Francisco: Jossey-Bass.

Gunes, Hatice, and Massimo Piccardi. 2006. "Assessing facial beauty through proportion analysis by image processing and supervised learning." *International Journal of Human-Computer Studies 64*(12): 1184–99.

Haidt, Jonathan, J. P. Seder, and S. Kesebir. 2008. "Hive psychology, happiness, and public policy." *Journal of Legal Studies 37.*

Hashmi, Shazia Iqbal, Chua Bee Seok, Murnizam Hj Halik, and Carmella E. Ading. 2012. "Mastery motivation and cognitive development among toddlers: A developmental perspective." http://www.ipedr.com/vol40/029-ICPSB2012-P10034.pdf.

Haslam, A., and Stephen Reicher. 2012. "Contesting the 'nature' of conformity: What Milgram and Zimbardo's studies really show." *PLoS Biology 10*(11), art. no. e1001426.

Hatfield, E., J. T. Cacioppo, and R. L. Rapson. 1993. "Emotional contagion." *Current Directions in Psychological Sciences 2*(3): 96–99.

Henrich, J., R. Boyd, S. Bowles, C. Camerer, E. Fehr, H. Gintis, and R. McElreath. 2001. "Cooperation, reciprocity and punishment in fifteen small-scale societies." *American Economic Review 91*(2), 73–78.

Howell, Ryan, Paulina Pchelin, and Ravi Iyer. 2012. "The preference for experiences over possessions: Measurement and construct validation of the experiential buying tendency scale." *Journal of Positive Psychology 7*(1): 57–71.

Hsu, Ming. 2005. "Neural systems responding to degrees of uncertainty in human decision-making." *Science 310*(5754): 1680–83. doi: 10.1126/science.1115327.

Hull, Clark L. 1934. "The rat's speed-of-locomotion gradient in the approach to food." *Journal of Comparative Psychology 17*(3): 393–422.

Iyengar, Sheena. 2010. *The Art of Choosing.* New York: Twelve.

Iyengar, Sheena, and M. R. Lepper. 2000. "When choice is demotivating: Can one desire too much of a good thing?" *Journal of Personality and Social Psychology 79*(6): 996–1006. doi: 10.1037/0022-3514.79.6.995.

Jonas, Eva, Jeff Schimel, Jeff Greenberg, and Tom Pyszczynski. 2002. "The Scrooge effect: Evidence that mortality salience increases prosocial attitudes and behavior." *Personality and Social Psychology Bulletin 28*(10): 1342–53. doi: 10.1177/014616702236834.

Jostmann, Nils, Daniël Lakens, and Thomas Schubert. 2009. "Weight as an embodiment of importance." *Psychological Science 20*(9), 1169–74. doi: 10.1111/j.1467-9280.2009.02426.x.

Kahneman, Daniel. 2011. *Thinking, Fast and Slow.* New York: Farrar, Straus and Giroux.

Kivetz, Ran, O. Urminsky, and Y. Zheng. 2006. "The goal-gradient hypothesis resurrected: Purchase acceleration, illusionary goal progress, and customer retention." *Journal of Marketing Research 43*(1): 39–58. doi: 10.1509/jmkr.43.1.39.

Knutson, Brian, C. Adams, G. Fong, and D. Hommer, D. 2001. "Anticipation of increasing monetary reward selectively recruits nucleus accumbens." *Journal of Neuroscience 21*(16): RC159.

Koo, Minjung, and A. Fishbach. 2010. "Climbing the goal ladder: How upcoming actions increase level of aspiration." *Journal of Personality and Social Psychology 99*(1): 1–13. doi: 10.1037/a0019443.

Krienen, Fenna M., Pei-Chi Tu, and Randy L. Buckner. 2010. "Clan mentality: Evidence that the medial prefrontal cortex responds to close others." *Journal of Neuroscience 30*(41): 13906–15. doi: 10.1523/JNEUROSCI.2180-10.2010.

Lally, Phillippa, C.H.M. van Jaarsveld, H.W.W. Potts, and J. Wardle. 2010. "How are habits formed: Modelling habit formation in the real world." *European Journal of Social Psychology, 40*(6): 998–1009. doi: 10.1002/ejsp.674.

Latané, Bibb, and J. Darley. 1970. *The Unresponsive Bystander.* Upper Saddle River, NJ: Prentice Hall.

Lefkowitz, M., R. R. Blake, and J. S. Mouton. 1955. "Status factors in pedestrian violation of traffic signals." *Journal of Abnormal and Social Psychology 51*(3): 704–6.

Lepper, Mark, David Greene, and Richard Nisbett. 1973. "Undermining children's intrinsic interest with extrinsic reward: A test of the 'overjustification' hypothesis." *Journal of Personality and Social Psychology 28*(1): 129–37.

Mason, Malia, Michael Norton, John Van Horn, Daniel Wegner, Scott Grafton, and C. Neil Macrae. 2007. "Wandering minds: The default network and stimulus-independent thought." *Science 315*(5810): 393–95. doi: 10.1126/science.1131295.

Meyer, D. E., J. E. Evans, E. J. Lauber, J. Rubinstein, L. Gmeindl, L. Junck, and R. A. Koeppe. 1997. "Activation of brain mechanisms for executive mental processes in cognitive task switching." *Journal of Cognitive Neuroscience,* vol. 9.

Milgram, Stanley. 1963. "Behavioral study of obedience." *Journal of Abnormal and Social Psychology 67*(4): 371–78. doi: 10.1037/h0040525.

Morgan, G. A., R. J. Harmon, and C. A. Maslin-Cole. 1990. "Mastery motivation: Definition and measurement." *Early Education and Development 1*(5): 318–39.

Pink, Daniel. (2009). *Drive: The Surprising Truth about What Motivates Us.* New York: Riverhead.

Provine, Robert. 2001. *Laughter: A Scientific Investigation.* New York: Penguin.

Roediger, Henry, and Bridgid Finn. "Getting it wrong: Surprising tips on how to learn." *Scientific American,* October 20, 2009. http://www.scientificamerican.com/article.cfm?id=getting-it-wrong.

Schwartz, Barry. 2005. *The Paradox of Choice: Why More Is Less.* New York: Harper Perennial.

Senay, Ibrahim, Dolores Albarracín, and Kenji Noguchi. 2010. "Motivating goal-directed behavior through introspective self-talk: The role of the interrogative form of simple future tense." *Psychological Science 21*(4): 499–504.

Shadmehr, Reza, and Henry H. Holcomb. 1997. "Neural correlates of memory motor consolidation." *Science 277*(5327): 821–25. doi: 10.1126/science.277.5327.821.

Shute, Valerie. 2007. *Focus on Formative Feedback.* http://www.ets.org/Media/Research/pdf/RR-07-11.pdf.

Singer, T., B. Seymour, J. O'Doherty, H. Kaube, R. J. Dolan, and C. Frith. 2004. "Empathy for pain involves the affective but not sensory component of pain." *Science 303*(5661): 1157–62. doi: 10.1126/science.1093535.

Siyang Luo, Shi Zhenhao, Zuo Xiangyu, and Han Shihui. 2012. "Reminder of death modulates anterior cingulate responses to the suffering of others." Presented at the Organization for Human Brain Mapping Conference.

Stephens, Greg, L. Silbert, and U. Hasson. 2010. "Speaker–listener neural coupling underlies successful communication." *Proceedings of the National Academy of Sciences.* doi: 10.1073/pnas.1008662107.

Teixeira, Thales, Michel Wedel, and Rik Pieters. 2012. "Emotion-induced engagement in internet video advertisements." *Journal of Marketing Research* 49(2): 144–59. doi: 10.1509/jmr.10.0207.

Thibodeau, P. H., and L. Boroditsky. 2011. "Metaphors we think with: The role of metaphor in reasoning." *PLoS ONE* 6(2): e16782. doi:10.1371/journal.pone.0016782.

Twain, Mark. *The Adventures of Tom Sawyer.*

Van Boven, L., M. Campbell, and T. Gilovich. 2010. "Stigmatizing materialism: On stereotypes and impressions of materialistic and experiential pursuits." *Personality and Social Psychology Bulletin* 36(4): 551–63. doi: 10.1177/014616721036279.

Vohs, Kathleen D., Nicole Mead, and Miranda Goode. 2006. "The psychological consequences of money." *Science* 314(5802): 1154–56. doi: 10.1126/science.1132491.

Walton, Gregory M., Geoffrey Cohen, David Cwir, and Steven Spencer. 2012. "Mere belonging: The power of social connections." *Journal of Personality and Social Psychology* 102(3): 513–32. doi: 10.1037/a0025731.

Wansink, Brian, Robert Kent, and Stephen Hoch. 1998. "An anchoring and adjustment model of purchase quantity decisions." *Journal of Marketing Research* 35(1): 71–81.

Williams, L. E., and John Bargh. 2008. "Experiencing physical warmth promotes interpersonal warmth." *Science* 322(5901): 606–7. doi: 10.1126/science.1162548.

Wilson, Timothy D. 2011. *Redirect: The Surprising New Science of Psychological Change.* New York: Little, Brown and Company.

Wilson, Timothy D. 2004. *Strangers to Ourselves: Discovering the Adaptive Unconscious.* Cambridge, MA: Harvard University Press.

Wiltermuth, Scott, and C. Heath. 2009. "Synchrony and cooperation." *Psychological Science* 20(1): 1–5. doi: 10.1111/j.1467-9280.2008.02253.x.

Worchel, Stephen, Jerry Lee, and Akanbi Adewole. 1975. "Effects of supply and demand on ratings of object value." *Journal of Personality and Social Psychology* 32(5): 906–14.

Wrosch, C., and J. Heckhausen. 2002. "Perceived control of life regrets: Good for young and bad for old adults." *Psychology and Aging* 17(2): 340–50.

Zak, Paul. 2012. *The Moral Molecule: The Source of Love and Prosperity.* New York: Dutton.

Index